New England
in a Nutshell

New England in a Nutshell

Quotations about the People,
Places, & Particulars of Life in the
Six New England States

The Editors of Commonwealth Editions

Commonwealth Editions

BEVERLY, MASSACHUSETTS

Library of Congress Cataloging-in-Publication Data
New England in a nutshell: quotations about the people, places & particulars of
life in the six New England states / the editors of Commonwealth Editions.
p. cm.
Includes index.
ISBN 1-899833-45-2
1. New England—Quotations, maxims, etc. I. Commonwealth Editions.
F4.5 .N49 2002
974—dc21   2002031498

Excerpts from "The Mountain" and "Two Tramps in Mud Time" from *The Poetry of
Robert Frost* edited by Edward Connery Lathem. Copyright 1930, © 1969 by Henry
Holt and Company, copyright 1936, 1958 by Robert Frost, copyright 1964, 1967 by
Lesley Frost Ballantine. Reprinted by permission of Henry Holt and Company LLC.
Excerpts from *New England: The Four Seasons*. Copyright © 1980 by Arthur Griffin.
Reprinted by permission of Houghton Mifflin Company. All rights reserved.
Excerpt from Cartalk.cars.com reprinted by permission of Tom Magliozzi.

Jacket design by Janet Theurer, Theurer/Briggs Design
Interior design by James F. Brisson
Printed in Canada

Published by Commonwealth Editions,
an imprint of Memoirs Unlimited, Inc.,
266 Cabot Street, Beverly, Massachusetts 01915
Visit our Web site: www.commonwealtheditions.com.

Table of Contents

NOTE FROM THE PUBLISHER   V

The New England Image   1

Weather and the Seasons   15

New England Character   41

Yankee Humor   73

The Educated Yankee   87

The New England Landscape   99

Boston   125

Yankee Cooking   143

Sense of Place   157

INDEX OF AUTHORS CITED   175

Note from the Publisher

IN PUBLISHING BOOKS OF NEW ENGLAND, we realized that we had seen no collection of quotations that describe just what we mean when we say "New England." What words, when read or spoken, evoke the New England image?

Debra Woodward asked for this book, and Penny Stratton brought it in on time. Among the editors who helped collect these words were Tim Lane, Linda Frahm, Liz Nelson, and Tim Clark. Edie Clark helped collect quotations, divided them into appropriate categories, and wrote the section introductions.

Janet Theurer and James F. Brisson developed designs and graphics that evoke New England as much as the quotations do. Jill Atkinson, Laura Tawater, Elizabeth Muller, Emma Stratton, and Sam Stratton helped with the myriad tasks of book production.

Webster Bull

August 2002

New England
in a Nutshell

The
New England
Image

A MIX OF ROMANTIC NOTIONS AND HARSH realities, the New England image was fostered by such early writers as Hawthorne and Thoreau, then more carefully crafted by the industry of Wallace Nutting, whose nostalgic images sold in early tourist shops. Nutting's books were among the first to promote the individual states. Magazines like *Yankee* further honed the image, which is part reality and part fantasy. The proud inhabitants of any region use words and images to convey their feelings about their home: so the words of people from the six northeastern states convey a certain image of New England.

Say the words *New England*, and one person will think of a white church spire and a village green; another will see a covered bridge or the Vermont hills in autumn; and still another will conjure up a farm along the Connecticut River. For me, the words evoke the sounds and smells of the sea, and the storms and the fogs that make life along the New England seacoast a good deal like living on an actual ship, subject to the whims of the weather.

—NATHANIEL BENCHLEY,
"The Sea," in *New England: The Four Seasons,* 1980

Above the white wainscoting, the pale-yellow walls were bare but for half a dozen amateur watercolors of the old farmhouse in different seasons. Beyond the cushioned windowseats and the colorless cotton curtains tied primly back I could see the bare limbs of big dark maple trees and fields of driven snow. Purity. Serenity. Simplicity. Seclusion. All one's concentration and flamboyance and originality reserved for the grueling, exalted, transcendent calling. I looked around and I thought, This is how I will live.

—PHILIP ROTH,
The Ghost Writer, 1979

Gaining access to the inner sanctum of Yankee society was a vital aspiration for Joseph and Rose Kennedy, but by the 1970s these old longings had become anachronistic. To outsiders, the exclusive Brahmin waltz evenings at the Ritz in Boston became equivalent to the polka nights at the Polish clubs.

—RICHARD D. BROWN,
Massachusetts: A History, 1978

I had known something of New England village life long before I made my home in the same county as my imaginary Starkfield; though, during the years spent there, certain of its aspects became much more familiar to me. Even before that final initiation, however, I had had an uneasy sense that the New England of fiction bore little . . . resemblance to the harsh and beautiful land as I had seen it.

—EDITH WHARTON,
introduction to *Ethan Frome, 1911*

About the mountains were ski slopes and hiking and horse trails, and in the south end of the valley, tennis courts, a skating rink, and a golf course. In other words, the village lived by the tourist—the well-heeled tourist. But few places in the country fused tourism and town life so well. In Woodstock, they were parts of the whole.

Any New England town worth its colonial salt has at least one bell cast in Paul Revere's foundry; like a DAR certificate, it's a touchstone of authenticity. Here, they boasted four.

—WILLIAM LEAST HEAT-MOON,
Blue Highways, 1982

North, South, East and West have been populated largely from New England, so that the seed-bed of New England was the seed-bed of the great American Republic, and of all that is likely to come of it.

—HARRIET BEECHER STOWE,
Oldtown Folks, 1869

New England is a finished place. . . . It is the first American civilization to be finished, to achieve stability in the conditions of its life. It is the first old civilization, the first permanent civilization in America.

—BERNARD DE VOTO,
Harper's magazine, March 1932

It seems odd that in all the years during which poets have sung of the lure of the great north woods, not one of them has made even passing mention of midges and black flies. . . . [It] gives rise to the suspicion that the poets of the great outdoors . . . have never been north of Portsmouth, N.H.

—KENNETH ROBERTS,
For Authors Only, 1935

6

There's little question that Vermont (particularly Vermont), Maine, Boston, and Cape Cod, are, together, responsible for the New England image. New Hampshire just doesn't fit in.

—JUDSON D. HALE, SR.,
"Vermont vs. New Hampshire,"
American Heritage, April 1992

We have helped create the Vermont image as a place where the skies are bluer, people work harder, the land is more fertile, and virtue springs from every brook. . . . The state has made money on that image.

—TOM SLAYTON,
editor of *Vermont Life* magazine,
quoted in *Yankee* magazine, October 1996

There were no curtains. Light saturated the immaculate rooms. In the kitchen was a wood-burning stove, an iron sink, gray-white walls, a basket of new peas. In lieu of electric lights, glass oil lamps were lined up, waiting for evening. "It looked like what Maine was *really* like, just as they found it," Wyeth remembers.

—RICHARD MERYMAN,
on Andrew Wyeth's first visit to Maine in 1939,
in *Andrew Wyeth: A Secret Life,* 1996

If it is no exaggeration to say that Deerfield is not so much a town as the ghost of a town, its dimness almost transparent, its quiet almost a cessation, it is essential to add that it is probably quite the most beautiful ghost of its kind, and with the deepest poetic and historic significance to be found in America. . . . It is, and will probably always remain, the perfect and beautiful statement of the tragic and creative moment when one civilization is destroyed by another.

—*WPA Guide to Massachusetts,* 1937

Some places, like some people, are magnets for adventure. Cape Cod is one. About anything that could happen anywhere has happened here. . . . Among its activities have been piracy, witchcraft, moon-cussing, bootlegging, bundling, fighting, and pioneering; and among those taking part have been Eskimos—though they moved away some time ago—Indians, Vikings, Pilgrims, Quakers, Hessians, and Portuguese, not to mention witches, mermaids, artists, and realtors.

—KATHARINE CROSBY,
Blue-Water Men and Other Cape Codders, 1946

Massachusetts! A word surrounded with an aura of hope! A state with a soul! There is gathered up into her name the brilliant pro-gram of a new world.

—WALLACE NUTTING,
Massachusetts Beautiful, 1923

One can believe anything on the Cape, a blessed relief from the doubts and uncertainties of the present-day turmoil of the outer world.

—THORNTON BURGESS,
Now I Remember, 1960

Look now at the wondrous traditional story of how this island [of Nantucket] was settled by the red-men. Thus goes the legend. In olden times an eagle swooped down upon the New England coast and carried off an infant Indian in his talons. With loud lament the parents saw their child borne out of sight over the wide waters. They resolved to follow in the same direction. Setting out in their canoes, after a perilous passage they discovered the island, and there they found an empty ivory casket,—the poor little Indian's skeleton

.   —HERMAN MELVILLE,
Moby-Dick, 1851

Somewhere along the line, Rhode Island became the standard by which all big things are compared. For reference, Alaska is 120 times the size of Rhode Island.

—"Road Trip—Western Canada and Alaska,"
June–October 1999, EarthRoamer.com

[Added to the reasons for moving] is the charm of New Canaan, a New England village at the end of a single track railroad with almost wild country in three directions, i.e. wild to an Easterner. An ideal place for bringing up children in the way they should go, girls anyhow.

—MAXWELL PERKINS,
on moving to New Canaan, Conn., in
Max Perkins, Editor of Genius by A. Scott Berg, 1978

New England haunted the minds of Americans, who tried to read its riddle, as if for their soul's good they must know what it meant. . . . For it meant much to Americans that this old region should fare well, as their palladium of truth, justice, freedom and learning. They could not rest until they were reconciled to it, and until it was reconciled to them.

—VAN WYCK BROOKS,
New England: Indian Summer, 1940

[By the last quarter of the 1800s] tourists sought out the isolated or remote parts of New England, looking for an imagined world of pastoral beauty, rural independence, virtuous simplicity, and religious and ethnic homogeneity. In these years, a trip to New England came to mean an escape from the conditions of modern urban industrial life, the very life New Englanders a generation earlier had been praised (and sometimes blamed) for creating.

—DONA BROWN,
Inventing New England, 1995

"Maybe they were triplets. You know, one of those things where three sisters marry brothers."

"That's the kind of stuff that's supposed to go on in New England," I agreed.

—SCOTT CORBETT,
We Chose Cape Cod, 1953

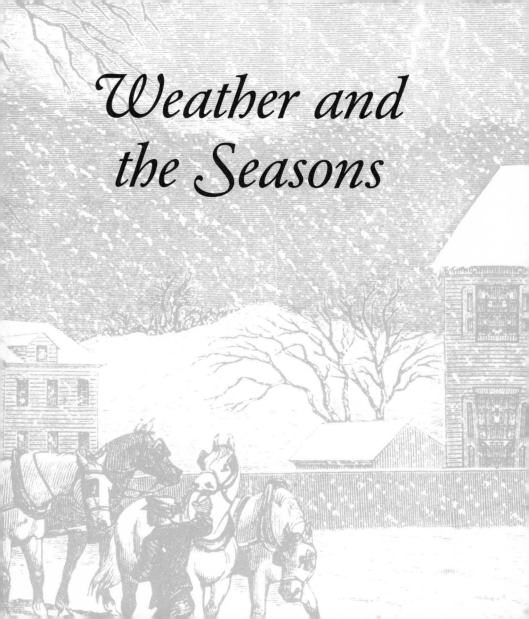

Weather and
the Seasons

PERHAPS NOWHERE IN THIS COUNTRY does weather provide more interest than in New England, where, as the old adage goes, if you don't like the weather, wait a minute and it will change. The California weatherman, if he exists at all, is a joke all his own. The maple syrup industry is in itself a celebration of a season virtually unknown in the rest of the country, and perhaps nowhere else on earth do travelers come in such numbers to regard the changing color of the leaves, a natural phenomenon created and produced by the simple turn of the weather and from which great profits are made. In New England, the weather is an entertainment all its own. Because if you can't change it, you might as well laugh about it.

[The Pilgrim Fathers] fell upon an ungenial climate, where there were nine months of winter and three months of cold weather and that called out the best energies of the men, and of the women too, to get a mere subsistence out of the soil, with such a climate. In their efforts to do that they cultivated industry and frugality at the same time—which is the real foundation of the greatness of the Pilgrims.

—ULYSSES S. GRANT,
    speech at New England Society dinner,
    December 22, 1880

Yes, one of the brightest gems in the New England weather is the dazzling uncertainty of it. There is only one thing certain about it: you are certain there is going to be plenty of it.

—MARK TWAIN,
    speech at New England Society dinner,
    December 22, 1876

17

New Hampshire is called the Granite State, because it is built entirely of granite, covered with a couple of inches of dirt. The New Hampshire farmer does not "till the soil," he blasts it. For nine months of the year he brings in wood, shovels snow, thaws out the pump, and wonders why Peary wanted to discover the North Pole. The other three months he blasts, plants, and hopes.

—WILL M. CRESSEY,
"The History of New Hampshire," 1920s

"A Vermont year is nine months winter and three months of damn poor sleddin'," commented an old Vermont farmer whose grand-father had survived 1816, "better known as 'eighteen hundred and froze to death.'"

—RAY BEARSE,
Vermont: A Guide to the Green Mountain State, 1968

Surely the framers of the Declaration of Independence did not have Vermonters in mind when they declared "all men are created equal," and the ordeal of winter in northern New England violates the national credo of equal justice for all.

   —CHARLES T. MORRISSEY,
    Vermont: A History, 1984

There has been more talk about the weather around here this year than common, but there has been more weather to talk about. For about a month now we have had solid cold—firm, business-like cold that stalked in and took charge of the countryside as a brisk housewife might take charge of someone else's kitchen in an emergency.

   —E. B. WHITE,
    on his first year at his Maine coast farm,
    One Man's Meat, 1944

Nowhere in the United States of America does the wheel of the seasons turn more brilliantly than in New England. Winter's blankets of white, the long-awaited buds of spring accompanied by the run of maple sap, summer's bouquets, and the magnificent palette of autumn: all are feasts for the senses, and lead to the characteristic New England feeling of existing in tandem with, and often at the mercy of, the great forces of nature.

—TOM SHACHTMAN,
The Most Beautiful Villages of New England, 1997

Some of us spend our lives preferring Fall to all the seasons . . . taking Spring only as prologue and Summer as the gently inclined platform leading all too slowly to the annual dazzle.

—DONALD HALL,
Seasons at Eagle Pond, 1987

Without going against Nature and absolutely defying the seasons, Rhode Island climate has as many variations as the solar system will permit.

—*WPA Guide to Rhode Island,* 1937

Decade after decade, artists came to paint the light of Provincetown, and comparisons were made to the lagoons of Venice and the marshes of Holland, but then the summer ended and most of the painters left, and the long dingy undergarment of the gray New England winter, gray as the spirit of my mood, came down to visit.

—NORMAN MAILER,
Tough Guys Don't Dance, 1984

A fresh fall of snow blanketed the asylum grounds—not a Christmas sprinkle, but a man-high January deluge, the sort that snuffs out schools and offices and churches, and leaves, for a day or more, a pure, blank sheet in place of memo pads, date books and calendars.

> —SYLVIA PLATH,
> *The Bell Jar,* 1963

Thirty below freezing! It was inconceivable till one stepped out into it at midnight and the shock of that clear, still air took away the breath as does a plunge into sea-water.

> —RUDYARD KIPLING
> on his arrival in Vermont, February 1892

Winter walks up and down the town swinging his censer, but no smoke or sweetness comes from it, only the sour, metallic frankness of salt and snow.

> —MARY OLIVER,
> *Winter Hours,* 1999

. . . .

But what would interest you about the brook,
It's always cold in summer, warm in winter.
One of the great sights going is to see
It steam in winter like an ox's breath,
Until the bushes all along its banks
Are inch-deep with the frosty spines and bristles—

. . . .

—ROBERT FROST,
"The Mountain," 1915

Winter was always the effort to live; summer was tropical license.

—HENRY ADAMS,
The Education of Henry Adams, 1918

23

What people really mean when they ask us if we live here the year 'round is "But good Lord! Certainly you don't stay in here during the winter? You must be crazy!" Well, all right, we're crazy. I would have thought so myself, before I tried it.

—LOUISE DICKINSON RICH,
We Took to the Woods, 1942

As I set out across the lake, about noontime, the cook, emerging to draw molasses from the barrel, warned me to "watch out for reefs"—rifts, that is, in the ice, where a warm current might have melted most of the way through. But the ice was solid, several inches thick, heavy enough to hold a team. There was only gladness in my heart as I started across the wide white plain toward the woods on the far-off shore.

—ROBERT SMITH,
My Life in the North Woods, 1986

24

It's March, the longest month of the year . . . . The Long March. The Death March. The March of Time, the March of Doom, the maddening thump-thump-thump of days in 4/4 time. No wonder we go a little crazy, or a lot, at this time of year. Our March entertainments have a desperate, hysterical quality.

—TIM CLARK,
"March Madness," *Yankee* magazine,
March 2002

March brings many things, but not hurricanes. But yesterday it brought a storm and a temperature drop, a farewell gesture from winter. The pipes froze again in the back part of the house. And as I viewed the solidly frozen bath mat in my shower, I felt I could do without any record-breaking statistics.

—GLADYS TABER,
The Stillmeadow Road, 1959

It was March in Vermont. Spring was filtering, seeping in like a wave in its tentative, halting, sometimes backtracking fashion— slow up the mountains, fast along the valleys.

—ARTURO VIVANTE,
  "The Sugar Maples," *Yankee* magazine, March 1983

Then "sugaring off" was a gala time, with parties in the "sugar bush," where dippers of syrup were poured into snow to harden for the guests. . . . Sweet, sour pickles were often served to whip up jaded appetites. They ate sugar between the buttered layers of pancakes four tiers thick; and songs were sung and jokes were cracked and even the most dour old farmer became genial at the thought that the long cold mountain winter was over and spring would soon be there.

—ERNEST POLE,
  on the sugar harvest after the 1938 hurricane,
  The Great White Hills of New Hampshire, 1946

Nathaniel Hawthorne, one of the most sensitive of our writers, wrote, "Happiness is a butterfly which when pursued is always just beyond your grasp, but which, if you will sit down quietly may alight upon you." Early spring is like that. It is scarcely more tangible than the weight of a butterfly on your outstretched hand, and unless you pause quietly you will not know it is there at all.

—ROY BARRETTE,
A Countryman's Journal, 1981

Spring, in Maine, is not exactly a date on the calendar. It comes when it gets good and ready, and before we see any summer folks we'll have another blizzard.

—JOHN GOULD,
Old Hundredth, 1987

27

It is mud season. God's yearly reminder to us of the clay from which we rose and to which we must return, hill people and Commoners alike.

—HOWARD FRANK MOSHER,
Where the Rivers Flow North, 1985

You know it's spring in Maine when . . .
The glass of water on your bedside table is not frozen when you wake up.
The mud sucks the shoes right off your feet.
There are more potholes in the road than cows.
The robins arrive wearing teeny, tiny LL Bean duck shoes.
The melting snowbanks reveal where you left the lawnmower last year.
The prices of lobstahs start going up.
July arrives.

—Answers to a question posed by the
Portland (Maine) Press Herald,
posted at MaineToday.com

The people of New England are by nature patient and forbearing, but there are some things which they will not stand. Every year they kill a lot of poets for writing about "Beautiful Spring." These are generally casual visitors who bring their notions of spring from somewhere else, and cannot, of course, know how the natives feel about spring.

—MARK TWAIN,
speech at New England Society dinner,
December 22, 1876

. . . .
The sun was warm but the wind was chill.
You know how it is with an April day
When the sun is out and the wind is still,
You're one month on in the middle of May.
But if you so much as dare to speak,
A cloud comes over the sunlit arch,
A wind comes off a frozen peak,
And you're two months back in the middle of March.

. . . .

—ROBERT FROST,
"Two Tramps in Mud Time," 1934

29

Pa Bean gets out of his old Chevy truck, workin' his legs stiffly over the icy yard. The aunties come behind him, dressed like for an American Legion dance, Auntie K. holdin' Auntie Hoover by the arm. It's been a cold spring and everywheres you look a robin is tryin' to peck a hole in the cementlike ground.

—CAROLYN CHUTE,
The Beans of Egypt, Maine, 1985

The sounds coming through our bedroom windows were ominous. We recognized the "crack-crash" punctuating the almost tangible silence as the noise of snapping, falling limbs. Two decades of New England woodland living had accustomed my wife and me to the winter ice storms and clinging wet snows that "trim" the pine trees. But this was early May in Massachusetts—a time of lilacs and apple blossoms.

—ROBERT C. COWEN,
on a May snowfall, *The American Land,* 1979

30

All gardening is an act of faith, but in no work in the garden is the chasm that faith must leap wider or deeper than in planting peas. In the North, where peas grow best, they are planted in April, which around here is called a spring month only out of courtesy to the equinox, much as you might call a mean, stingy, and detested family acquaintance "Uncle" Adolf.

—CASTLE FREEMAN, JR.,
Spring Snow, 1995

Now I know summer is here, no matter how cold it is at night, for when I went out to the car this morning, the windshield was dusted with orange and the whole shiny dark blue of the body was powdered. The pine pollen has come! This is a thick, almost oily deposit that penetrates everything. If you close a room and lock the windows, the sills will be drifted with the pollen the next morning. The floors turn orange.

—GLADYS TABER,
My Own Cape Cod, 1971

31

The first "hot" day of the season has happened. I put "hot" in quotation marks because in Maine the term is strictly relative. Most people can live in Maine for years without learning what hot really means; some of them may never learn unless they leave the state.

—JOHN COLE,
In Maine, 1974

Summer is the time when one sheds one's tensions with one's clothes, and the right kind of day is jeweled balm for the battered spirit. A few of those days and you can become drunk with the belief that all's right with the world.

—ADA LOUISE HUXTABLE,
on vacationing in New England,
New York Times, September 1977.

"No-see-um" was an Indian word—red skin vulnerable as white. To the early Indian, coming here to make a warm-weather camping trip would have seemed the act of a fool: Thoreau, with his veil, his smoke from rotting logs; we, with our Off and our Cutter. When the tribes lived here . . . they left in the summer. When the black-flies, the mosquitoes, and the no-see-ums hatched, the Indians departed, and they did not come back until the bugs were gone.

—JOHN McPHEE,
The Survival of the Bark Canoe, 1975

Summer on a Maine island means a host of rainy mornings, even days, spent in front of the fireplace. The gray light in the window, the feathery murmur of rain on the roof, the banshee wail of the fog siren down past Doughty's Landing at the naval station, the reso-nant splash of rainwater tumbling into the rain barrels—the signs were there the moment I woke up, huddled in a bundle of flannel sheets and army blankets.

—JOHN THORNE,
Simple Cooking, 1980

A danger exists of confusing the Vineyard with my children's child-hood, which time has swallowed, or with Paradise, from which we have been debarred by well-known angels. Let's not forget the rainy days, the dull days, the cranky-making crowding, and the moldy smell summer furniture gives off when breezes don't blow through the screen door that one keeps meaning to fix, though it's the land-lord's responsibility.

—JOHN UPDIKE,
"Going Barefoot," *On the Vineyard II,* 1990

A season peculiar to New England is that known as the Indian sum-mer, which occurs in October and continues only two or thre weeks. It comes after the early frosts, when the wind is southwest, and the air is delightfully mild and sweet. The sky is then singularly transparent, pure and beutiful, and the fleecy clouds are bright with color. The Indians believed the season to be caused by a wind that was sent from the southwestern god Cautantowwit, who was regarded as superior to all other beings in benevolence and power, and the one to whom their souls went when they departed from the earthly body.

—SIDNEY PERLEY,
Historic Storms of New England, 1891

34

Autumn is the American Season. In Europe the leaves turn yellow or brown, and fall. Here they take fire on the trees and hang there flaming.

—ARCHIBALD MACLEISH,
in *New England: The Four Seasons,* 1980

Maine has two seasons. Winter and August.

—WILL M. CRESSEY,
"The History of Maine," 1920s

It was a radiant October day: Connecticut suggested an outrageous show-off, the low hills overflowing with autumnal brilliance, eruptions of golden leaves, friezes of crimson, the pines maintaining their sober greenness amid the blaze like sentinels.

All this last glory of the growing season was nevertheless contained, neat, firmly—for centuries now—under control: this was New England.

—JOHN KNOWLES,
A Stolen Past, 1983

The fields pulsate yet with the sound of cricket and cicada. . . .
[The] ponds lie there misty, warm, seductive. One day camouflaged
as summer, fall can easily toss off this disguise and appear as
prophet: cold wet, angry.

—ANNE BERNAYS,
"Fall," in *New England: The Four Seasons,* 1980

Living here, inside the drama, we watch the spectrum turn, a wide
prism of the natural world that revolves at the pace of the turning of
the earth. That tree that was tinted red yesterday is more intense
today and then, gradually, like the flame turned up on a lamp, it's
brilliant, unimaginably red.

—EDIE CLARK,
"The Garden at Chesham Depot,"
Yankee magazine, October 1998

There have been times . . . when the weather has mobilized its forces and ripped New England wide open. These times are the hurricanes.

—EDWARDS PARKS,
The American Land, 1979

The gathering-in time stirs every living fiber in me. Picking apples was the part of farm work that really delighted me; though gathering the corn was fun. Why no great poet has made one or both of these immortal in his verse is a puzzle. The Roman singers of the olive had no such theme.

—WALLACE NUTTING,
Wallace Nutting's Biography, 1936

November had come; the crops were in, and barn, buttery, and bin were overflowing with the harvest that rewarded the summer's hard work. The big kitchen was a jolly place just now, for in the great fireplace roared a cheerful fire; on the walls hung garlands of dried apples, onions, and corn; up aloft from the beams shone crook-necked squashes, juicy hams, and dried venison—for in those days deer still haunted the deep forests, and hunters flourished. Savory smells were in the air; on the crane hung steaming kettles, and down among the red embers copper saucepans simmered, all sugges-tive of some approaching feast.

—LOUISA MAY ALCOTT,
An Old Fashioned Thanksgiving, 1888

[It's] the only fault that I have with Maine, the water is just too damn cold.

—ARTHUR GRIFFIN,
New England: The Four Seasons, 1980

Vermonters who try to fly in and out of this state on airplanes when the weather is unsettled know how it feels to be a piece of lettuce in a tossed salad.

—CHARLES T. MORRISSEY,
Vermont: A History, 1984

The most serious charge which can be brought against New England is not Puritanism but February.

—JOSEPH WOOD KRUTCH,
"February," *The Twelve Seasons*, 1949

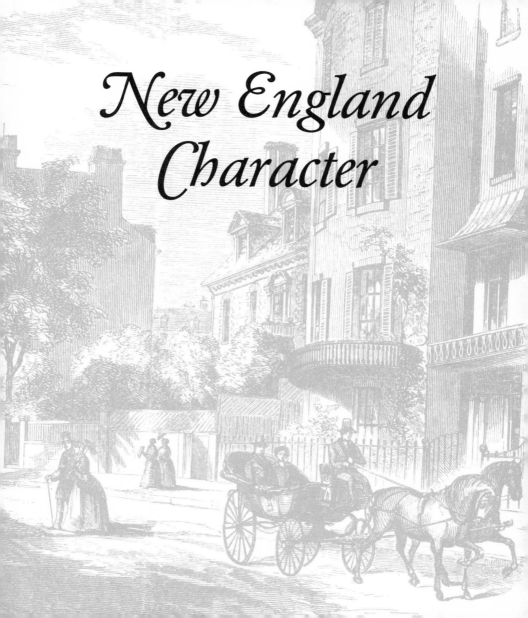

New England Character

TACITURN, FLINTY, HARDWORKING, SHREWD, ENTERPRISING, FRUGAL, GRITTY. A string of words could be used to describe the personality of the Yankee. Most of these traits can be traced to New Englanders' ethnic roots and to the severe nature of the land and of the climate. A great stew of ethnicity—Irish, Scottish, Polish, English, Italian, French, and more—combined to create the peculiarities of speech and the characteristics that we think of when we think New England. A fascination to writers, the character of the New Englander has been the subject of many literary classics, from *Moby-Dick* to *The Beans of Egypt, Maine.*

Do you know how I got through the change of life? I went out and built a camp from driftwood on the outer shores of Cutler.

—RUTH FARRIS,
from her weekly column in the
Machias Valley (Maine) News Observer, 1994

Dear Jack: In looking over the monthly statement from Choate, I notice there is a charge of $10.80 for suit pressing for the month of March. It strikes me that this is very high and while I want you to keep looking well, I think that if you spent a little more time picking up your clothes instead of leaving them on the floor, it wouldn't be necessary to have them pressed so often.

—JOSEPH P. KENNEDY,
to his 14-year-old son, John F. Kennedy, 1932

They can have their granite. I'll take the good clean dirt for me. I've known a lot of granite workers of course. I used to know all the old-timers and they was good men. I don't know so many now, but the ones I knew I liked. Maybe they lived faster'n a farmer does. They have to, by God, because they don't last so long. I never blamed em for carrying on the way they did. They was good-hearted fellers, good fellers to talk to. They might raise hell but it wasn't out of meanness. The work they do, the life they lead, a man's got to have some way to let go and get away from it.

> —"HENRY ERIKSON,"
> Barre, Vermont, farmer, quoted in *First Person America,*
> edited by Ann Banks, 1980

YANKEE, n. In Europe, an American. In the Northern States of our Union, a New Englander. In the Southern States the word is unknown. (See DAMNYANK.)

> —AMBROSE BIERCE,
> *The Devil's Dictionary*, 1911

Independent as a hog on ice.

—Vermont expression

A farmer . . . has an enormous innate need to simply hold still, to keep what he's got, to limit his greed to what he can keep. . . . What's the use of owning more than you can plough, or hay, or cut into sawlogs or pulp or firewood in wintertime, or drive spiles into to bleed out maple sap in sugar time? No use, at all. In the Connecticut Valley, this Yankee trait has saved a lot of beauty.

—EVAN HILL,
The Connecticut River, 1972

New England likes to think it has a civilization based on character. The South likes to think it has a character based on civilization. A big difference.

—HENRY ALLEN,
"The Character of Summer,"
The Washington Post Magazine, July 14, 1991

Let's see, what did we do for recreation? I don't know. Worked, I guess.

—WILLIE AMES,
quoted in *The Salt Book,* edited by Pamela Wood, 1977

I conversed with a young lobster fisherman who gets up at 5 in the morning and home again from the sea at 3 in the afternoon. I asked him if he liked lobstering. "You get used to it," was his reply.

—EARL THOLLANDER,
Back Roads of New England, 1974

Use it up,
Wear it out,
Make do
Or do without.

—Yankee adage

46

New Hampshire
Live Free or Die

—Slogan on New Hampshire
license plates

There is nothing that a New-Englander so nearly worships as an
argument.

—HENRY WARD BEECHER,
Proverbs from Plymouth Pulpit, 1887

It is a hoary New England tradition to keep track of where famous
people slept instead of something they might have done while
conscious.

—ANDREW H. MALCOLM,
U.S. 1: America's Original Main Street, 1991

47

[Lee Totman] is more than just a good farmer. . . . He doesn't waste moves. He is always set up for the job he needs to do. He plans only as much as his equipment and help permit. He takes shortcuts where they pay and lavishes attention where that pays better. His manure truck is an old unregistered jalopy; his equipment shed is made of old telephone poles and sheet tin.

—MARK KRAMER,
Three Farms, 1980

The Yankee girl is the rose laurel, whose blossoms no garden flower ever excelled in rosy delicacy and gracefulness of form, but whose root asks neither garden-bed nor gardener's care, but will take for itself strong hold where there is a handful of earth in the cleft of a rock.

—HARRIET BEECHER STOWE,
"The Yankee Girl," 1842

The New Hampshire girls who came to Lowell were descendants of the sturdy backwoodsmen who settled that State. . . . Their grandmothers had suffered the hardships of frontier life . . . when the beautiful valleys of the Connecticut and the Merrimack were threaded with Indian trails from Canada to the white settlements. Those young women . . . were earnest and capable; ready to undertake anything that was worth doing.

> —LUCY LARCOM,
> *A New England Girlhood,* 1889

In a society still under the sway of Calvinist attitudes, as were the rural communities of New England, a degree of disgrace would attach to the condition of being poor. . . . Thus, to "go on the town" would be viewed as an ignominy to be avoided if at all possible— and of course it would be a public ignominy, for everyone knew who the poor were and often they would be discussed by name in town meeting.

> —PERRY WESTBROOK,
> *The New England Town in Fact and Fiction,* 1982

"You goin' to get your deer?" I am asked by every man I meet—and they all wait for an answer. My deer-slaying program is a matter of considerable local import, much to my surprise. It is plain that I now reside in a friendly community of killers, and that until I open fire myself they cannot call me brother.

> —E.B. WHITE,
> on living in Maine, *One Man's Meat,* 1944

My grandfather was the son of a sea captain in the North Atlantic trade and he had inherited the habits of the quarterdeck: he not only spoke out; he spoke out in the wind's teeth.

> —ARCHIBALD MACLEISH,
> "A Lay Sermon for the Hill Towns," 1978

The New England conscience . . . does not stop you from doing what you shouldn't—it just stops you from enjoying it.

> —CLEVELAND AMORY,
> *New York,* May 5, 1980

All Yankees are known for their frugality, I suppose, but well-to-do ✓
Yankees most perfectly embody the idea. In no other part of the
country are the rich so cheap.

> —JOHN SEDGWICK,
>   "In No Other Part of the Country Are the Rich So Cheap,"
>   *Yankee* magazine, September 1991

Henry was his own man; in his battered old truck, with tottering load
of hay on it . . . he implied an old-fashioned resourcefulness and independence, which we could praise even if we couldn't emulate.

> —FRANKLIN BURROUGHS,
>   "Of Moose and Moose Hunter," 1991

Perhaps nowhere in the world can be found more unlovely wicked-
ness—a malignant, bitter, tenacious hatred of good—than in New
England. The good are very good and the bad are very bad.

> —HENRY WARD BEECHER, 1868

The next night an indignation meeting was held in Boston's Old South Meeting House, a prime example of one of the most original and durable of New England colonial institutions: the church considered not only as a place of worship but as a court of law and a social center and the very hub of political life."

—ALISTAIR COOKE,
on the response to the "Boston Massacre," *America,* 1973

[Amherst is] the last place in America where you can find people who still think *politically correct* is a compliment . . . probably the only place in the United States where men can wear berets and not get beaten up.

—MADELEINE BLAIS,
In These Girls, Hope Is a Muscle, 1995

There are houses in Gloucester where grooves have been worn into the floorboards by women pacing past an upstairs window, looking out to sea. . . . If fishermen lived hard, it was no doubt because they died hard as well.

—SEBASTIAN JUNGER,
The Perfect Storm, 1997

There is no pleasing New Englanders, my dear, their soil is all rocks and their hearts are bloodless absolutes.

—JOHN UPDIKE,
Buchanan Dying, 1974

53

By 1920, we had begun to use skis fairly consistently instead of snowshoes at Tolman Pond. A Norwegian family who visited at the farm introduced us to bindings that stayed put reasonably well, and to ski wax and proper poles, and soon we were exploring the magical mysteries of the Christiania turn. . . . But it was all strictly for fun and nobody dreamed a business might be made out of it. In fact the older generation did its best to discourage us from such a dangerous and silly waste of time.

   —NEWTON F. TOLMAN,
    North of Monadnock, 1957

The only thing that was dispensed free to the old New Bedford whalemen was a Bible. A well-known owner of one of that city's whaling fleets once described the Bible as the best cheap investment a shipowner could make.

   —*WPA Guide to Massachusetts,* 1937

"You've spent most of your life right here in this house?"

"I and Continental Telephone, born in this very house. Hope to die here. And why not? First and last memories in the same place. My parents kept me as a baby in a box under the counter, down with the Uneeda biscuits."

—WILLIAM LEAST HEAT-MOON,
Blue Highways, 1982

A man was cleaning the attic of an old house in New England and he found a box which was full of tiny pieces of string. On the lid of the box there was an inscription in an old hand: "String too short to be saved."

—DONALD HALL,
String Too Short To Be Saved, 1981

The world of New England is in that house—spidery, like crackling skeletons rotting in the attic—dry bones. It's like a tombstone to sailors lost at sea, the Olson ancestor who fell from the yardarm of a square-rigger and was never found. It's the doorway of the sea to me, of mussels and clams and sea monsters and whales.

—ANDREW WYETH,
on the home of his model Christina Olson, in
Andrew Wyeth: A Secret Life by Richard Meryman, 1996

Basically, there are two New Englands, northern and southern, with plenty of shared schizophrenia between them. . . . The Connecticut Yankee and the Maine Yankee may both trade on rurality for their wit, but the one is garrulous and the other taciturn. When the Bostonian tells a story the Vermonter becomes an ignorant hayseed; when the Vermonter tells a story the Bostonian is a pompous ignoramus. Usually in such a match there's no contest; the Vermonter will inevitably prevail.

—JIM BRUNELLE,
The Best of New England Humor, 1990

Hard work was not only necessary, but it was also noble; and to avoid it would lead to disgrace, dishonor, and probably, eventually, to Hell itself. If a true Yankee ran out of work, he was expected to look for more.

—LEWIS HILL,
Fetched-Up Yankee, 2001

The three Puritan virtues were Sabbath-keeping, Chastity and Thrift, and we're still pretty thrifty. . . . Early New Englanders were very good people—but not the sort you'd like to spend a week-end with.

—ELEANOR EARLY,
A New England Sampler, 1940

I don't know whether it was the climate, or the water, or what it was, but these Vermonters have always been the most cantankerous, independent, stubborn folks in America. They just never would belong to *anybody*. England, France, New York, Massachusetts, New Hampshire would bargain and traffic and trade Vermont around; and then, just as they had got everything settled to everybody's satisfaction, Vermont would gum up the whole trade by refusing to be traded.

—WILL M. CRESSEY,
"The History of Vermont," 1920s

[My grandmother] had been born and brought up in a great, flat-roofed Palladian house with fanlight windows over the doors and yard-wide pumpkin-pine paneling, in the southwest corner of Maine. There she had absorbed simultaneously the frugality and the classicism of Down East New England. She could make soap and translate Horace with equal facility and mordant effect.

—ROBERT K. LEAVITT,
The Chip on Grandma's Shoulder, 1954

Inhabitants of this [Connecticut] valley . . . are so remote from a market as to be perfectly free from that sense of inferiority customarily felt by the body of people who live in the neighborhood of large cities. Hence a superior spirit of personal independence is generated and cherished.

—TIMOTHY DWIGHT,
Travels in New England and New York, 1821–22

In person [John Brown] was lean, strong, and sinewy, of the best New England mold, built for time of trouble and fitted to grapple with the flintiest hardships.

—FREDERICK DOUGLASS,
The Life and Times of Frederick Douglass, 1892

There is great equality in the People of this State—Few or no oppulent Men and no poor—great similatude in their buildings—the general fashion of which is a Chimney (always Stone or Brick) and door in the middle, with a stair case fronting the latter . . . two flush Stories with a very good shew of Sash & glass Windows. . . [and] a back shed which seems to be added as the family encreases.

—GEORGE WASHINGTON,
on Massachusetts, 1789

In New England there persists the character which is the basis of quality.

—JONATHAN DANIELS,
A Southerner Discovers New England, 1940

In the Hancock, New Hampshire, historical society . . . is the town coffin, once used to bury the poor. (Thrifty Yankees, using the same coffin, and thriftier still—for years it was used as a chicken feeder on a farm.)

—HOWARD MANSFIELD,
In the Memory House, 1993

I was born on the kitchen table on the top floor of a three-decker wooden house on Merrick Street in West Springfield, Massachusetts. Two days later, my mother was back at her work. That's the way it was done in that kind of neighborhood, at that time.

—LEO DUROCHER,
Nice Guys Finish Last, 1976

Three days we call a visit. According to established usage, if our friends stay more than three days it is expected they will do chores night and morning.

—HENRY STEVENS of Vermont,
in a letter to Edward Fairbanks, October 10, 1860

In our town, we like to know the facts about everybody.

—THORNTON WILDER,
Our Town, 1938

I see no truth at all in the myth that New Englanders are taciturn—they love gossip as well as anyone I ever knew—the talk takes place mostly on neutral ground: in stores and barnyards, at auctions and church suppers. Your home is private.

—NOEL PERRIN,
The Amateur Sugar Maker, 1972

He loved winter more than the other seasons, loved a tender snow-fall, loved the savage north wind and the blinding light off a frozen lake, loved most a blizzard, which he faced head-on like a bison. He would not admit these things, however, because in his superstition he believed that by revealing desires about sacred subjects, such as weather and seasons, you would likely receive the opposite of what you wanted.

—ERNEST HEBERT,
The Dogs of March, 1979

A genuine New Englander learned by example never to take anything for granted. Once, when I remarked that it was a nice day, my Uncle Henry looked up at the sky, turned in every direction, and seeing there wasn't a cloud anywhere, took the pipe from his mouth and finally conceded, "Well, maybe."

—LEWIS HILL,
Fetched-up Yankee, 2001

New England has a great many houses of worship, at least in part because it was settled by people who were unhappy with the Church of England, or with Rome, or with Martin Luther; or who simply had a scheme of their own they wanted to try out—usually having to do with wearing black clothes and making sure everyone behaved.

—C. MICHAEL CURTIS,
Contemporary New England Stories, 1992

The peculiarity of the New England hermit has not been his desire to get near to God but his anxiety to get away from man.

—HAMILTON WRIGHT MABIE (1845–1916)

Vermonters are really something quite special and unique . . . . This state bows to nothing: the first legislative measure it ever passed was "to adopt the laws of God . . . until there is time to frame better."

—JOHN GUNTHER,
Inside USA, 1947

In the end, Harriet Beecher Stowe looked on the phenomenon of slavery through the clean moral categories of the Yankee reformer, and what she saw was a race of children being abused by a race of fiends.

—ANDREW DELBANCO,
Required Reading, 1997

Transcendentalism has been called the inevitable flowering of the Puritan spirit. But Puritanism does not necessarily bear blossoms, and the fruit thereof is often gnarled and bitter. In New England, however, the soil was conserved by a bedrock of character, mellowed by two centuries of cultivation, and prepared by Unitarianism. New England Federalism checked the flow of sap, fearful lest it feed flowers of Jacobin red. There was just time for a gorgeous show of blossom and a harvest of wine-red fruit, between this late frost and the early autumn blight of the Civil War.

—SAMUEL ELIOT MORISON,
The Oxford History of the American People, 1965

As a child of Maine, he knew better than to learn to swim in the water; the Maine water, in Wilbur Larch's opinion, was for summer people and lobsters.

—JOHN IRVING,
Cider House Rules, 1985

65

If the antique New England spirit has a sovereign flower, it must be the rhodora, a wild shrub . . . that . . . produces profuse, extravagant flowers that spill down off of branches which as yet show no leaves. The flowers are pink, red, purple—the colors of a tropical garden. You're a little startled to come upon that kind of show in the waste, remote environs where the rhodora briefly blows. It's that surprise, that contrast of display and diffidence that expresses a characteristic of the New England mind.

—CASTLE FREEMAN, JR.,
The Old Farmer's Almanac, 2002

Between five o'clock and sunset, society drove up and down Bellevue Avenue and Ocean Drive. . . . The two-way procession passed and repassed. It was said: the first time you met a friend, you made a ceremonious bow; the second time, you smiled; the third, you looked away.

—BERTRAM LIPPINCOTT,
on Newport in the early 20th century,
Indians, Privateers and High Society, 1961

66

Even after thirty years, I still think New Englanders sound funny, that they expect too much of the Red Sox, that their religiosity is more procedural than deeply felt, and that their highways were built with the conviction that automobiles could not possibly replace the horse-drawn buggy, and therefore need not be wide, permanent, or especially well-designed.

—C. MICHAEL CURTIS,
Contemporary New England Stories, 1992

In short, the steady habits of a great portion of the inhabitants [of Connecticut] . . . seem to be laziness, low bickerings, and whoring.

—ALEXANDER WILSON, 1808

The Maine Yankee is not nearly as taciturn as a stranger might at first consider him, but it is a rule that words are not to be wasted.

—*WPA Maine: A Guide "Down East,"* 1937

67

[The blacksmith] is good-natured and good-hearted, fond of joke, and shaking his jolly sides with frequent laughter. His conversation has much strong, unlettered sense, imbued with humor, as everybody's talk is in New England.

—NATHANIEL HAWTHORNE,
"The Prosperous Blacksmith," 1838

Like many other families imbued with the Puritan tradition, the Apleys have not been in the habit of destroying letters or papers.

—JOHN P. MARQUAND,
The Late George Apley, 1936

Yankees are what they always were.

—ROBERT FROST,
"Brown's Descent, or the Willy-nilly Slide," 1920

Any woman, going softly to her neighbor to break the news of her husband lost in the Arctic ice, might in some dark hour drop her head upon her neighbor's shoulder in hearing of a son drowned off the banks or slain by South Sea islanders.

—KATHARINE LEE BATES,
Historic Towns of New England, 1898

[Stick the remnant of each bar of soap onto the next bar.] Theoretically, some of the atoms will remain in my bar until my very last shower. When I'm gone, my son can continue to use the bar as I have . . . and thus shall my zealous frugality be passed down from generation to generation as long as my descendants shall lather up.

—Suggestion from a reader of
The Tightwad Gazette, Leeds, Maine

Look. And smell. Breathe deeply. Feel the air; touch it now and sense its purity, its vigor, its super-constant juvenation (that supposedly has given Vermonters their long life—if you discount their stubbornness).

—EVAN HILL,
The Connecticut River, 1972

I have heard New Englanders say that they have an affinity for Box[wood]—that it exerts power like a hereditary memory, and affects them with an almost hypnotic force. This is not felt by everyone, but only by those who have loved Box for centuries, in the persons of their ancestors.

—ELEANOR EARLY,
A New England Sampler, 1940

Most people believe . . . that any problem in the world can be solved if you know enough; most Vermonters know better.

—JOHN GARDNER,
October Light, 1976

Tobacco is an Indian weed,
From the Devil it doth proceed,
It picks your pockets, burns your clothes,
And makes a chimney of your nose.

—Pilgrim rhyme

There was a curious New England custom . . . called Bundling, which was love-making under peculiar circumstances. . . . Boys and girls who bundled went to bed together, with their clothes on, and stayed until morning. Sometimes they got married afterward. And sometimes they didn't. . . . Many Mayflower Descendants have a bundling ancestry, though they never mention it.

—ELEANOR EARLY,
A New England Sampler, 1940

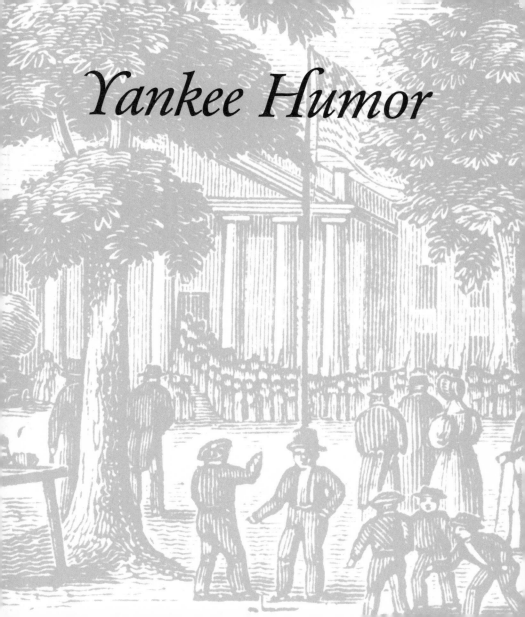

Yankee Humor

WHAT'S FUNNY IN NEW ENGLAND is what is not said, the short, pithy jokes, the pauses, the quick rejoinders. New Englanders are not thought of as a people who laugh heartily or spend much time having fun. But, with their quick wits and stony expressions, they can make a lot of other people laugh. Fred Allen, Bert and I, Bob and Ray, even Jay Leno—all have given voice to this peculiar brand of humor, very much worth celebrating.

My wife died five o'clock this morning, spent the rest of the morning making her coffin. Ran out of nails. Twice. Split three covers before I got the fourth one nailed down tight. Bruised my thumb with the hammer. Pulled my back lifting the coffin into the wagon. Broke the halter as the horse pulled the wagon out of the barn, so we had to go into town pulling crooked. Got out of control going down that last hill and my wife just shot right off the back of the wagon. Crashed through the post office window. I jumped off, run inside to make sure no one was injured. There was Tut Tuttle, the postman, staring at me through the stamp window. Said: "Lucky I had the grating down."

"Sure was," I replied.

"Did you pass the preacher and the undertaker heading out your place this morning?" he asked.

"I said, 'Tut, I come into town to see if I couldn't find them.'

"He said, 'I guess you missed them.'

"I said, 'I guess I did.'

"I said, 'Tut you know—my day's been one long fizzle from beginning to end.'"

> —MARSHALL DODGE (Bert and I)
> at a gathering of Maine storytellers, 1978 Maine Festival,
> Brunswick, Maine

75

Five crows, frock-coated in dignity, have arrived and sit upright and still on a bough. One thinks, "Oh, beloved symbols of New England" or "Drat those birds," depending upon whether one is planning a poem or a cornfield.

—RICHARD F. MERRIFIELD,
Monadnock Journal, 1975

[A] Connecticut River Valley farmer . . . was told that his farm . . . was really in New Hampshire, instead of in Vermont as he'd always thought. "Thank God," he said, "I didn't think I could stand another one of those Vermont winters."

—EVAN HILL,
The Connecticut River, 1972

Question: What's the difference between a Fenway frank and one bought at Yankee Stadium?
Answer: You can't buy Fenway franks in October.

—Boston lament

Even my children, though born here, would not be called Vermonters by most members of long-time Bristol families. (My neighbors might well respond, if I put the question to them, with the old Vermont joke: If the cat has kittens in the oven, does that make them biscuits?)

—JOHN ELDER,
Reading the Mountains of Home, 1971

Anyone who has lived in Rhode Island for any length of time is familiar with the custom of giving directions according to where something used to be.

—MICHAEL E. BELL,
Rhode Island state folklorist

Question: How many Vermonters does it take to change a lightbulb? *Answer:* Three. One to change it and two to argue over why the old one was better.

—Vermont joke

It is said that Jim Thorpe once hit a ball into an adjoining state when playing semi-professional ball in Texas. I don't know what the big deal is; they do it all the time in Rhode Island.

> —JIM HART,
> "Swing for the Fences," speech given in
> Des Moines, July 25, 2001

A Texan is bragging to a New Englander. "In Texas," he drawls, "you can get on a train, ride all day long, and still be in Texas by nightfall."

"So what?" replies the Yankee, "We have slow trains in Rhode Island, too."

> —Old joke

It appears to be the firm conviction of many of the Maine citizenry that since there's no legal way to keep people from coming to Maine, the least that can be done is to make it as inconvenient as possible.

> —LEW DIETZ,
> on the end of passenger train service to Maine,
> *Night Train at Wiscasset Station,* 1977

78

By 1760 Newport was humming with industry. As one old history states, "Newport was not the headquarters for piracy, sugar, smuggling, rum, molasses, and slaves." But time has worked wonders. There is very little molasses or sugar used there now.

—WILL M. CRESSEY,
"The History of Rhode Island," 1920s

New England humor more or less starts . . . with the lost tourist or city person asking directions of some grizzled old Maine or Vermont country native and receiving in return a devastating one-liner.

—JUDSON D. HALE, SR.,
Inside New England, 1982

Here in Maine we draw from pioneer beginnings to maintain that pies are to cut wood on. That is, you tuck away a piece of pie and it will sustain you at your work, whereas food that digests on you is a sham and imposter.

—JOHN GOULD,
Old Hundredth, 1987

Late every night in Connecticut, lights go out in the cities and towns, and citizens by tens of thousands proceed zestfully to break the law.

> —*Time* magazine, on Connecticut law against
> contraceptives, March 10, 1961

I see that *Life* Magazine calls the New England town meeting the quintessence of democracy; but one of my neighbors, who has probably attended more of them than the editors of *Life,* had another name for it. "Well," he said, as we climbed into our car balancing a pot of baked beans wrapped in a paper bag, "here we go to the Chase & Sanborn hour."

> —E. B. WHITE,
> *One Man's Meat,* 1944

"Senator, how did you get your start in life?" asked the reporter. "I was born on a hillside farm in Vermont," said the eminent statesman, "and at an early age I rolled down."

> —Quoted from the *Chicago Tribune* in *Expansion: Vermont's
> Industrial Magazine,* 1905

An old man is sitting on the steps of the general store on a fine spring day. A stranger comes along and tips his hat and comments on the beauty of the day. He pauses, searching for something more to say, and finally he says, "Bet you've seen a lot of changes around here." To which the old man replies, "Ayup. And I've been against every one of them."

—EDIE CLARK,
"Pure Vermont," *Yankee* magazine, October 1996

Question: Does it matter which road I take to Millinocket?
Answer: Not to me it don't.

—Old Maine joke

Summer person: "Nice little town, so old and quaint. But I suppose you have a lot of oddballs, too."
Native: "Oh, yes, quite a few. You see 'em around. But they're mostly gone after Labor Day."

—Adapted from JUDSON D. HALE, SR.,
Inside New England, 1982

The circulation manager of *Down East* magazine sent a letter to Abner Mason of Damariscotta, Maine, notifying him that his subscription had expired. The notice came back a few days later with a scrawled message: "So's Abner."

—JUDSON D. HALE, SR.,
Inside New England, 1982

The Senses taker in our town being taken sick he deppertised me to go out for him one day, and as he was too ill to giv me informashun how to perceed, I was consekently compelled to go it blind. . . . But it didn't work. I got into a row at the fust house I stopt to, with some old maids. Disbelievin the answers they giv in regard to their ages I endevered to look at their teeth, same as I do with hosses, but they floo into a violent rage and tackled me with brooms and sich. Takin the senses requires experiunse, like any other bizniss.

—ARTEMUS WARD, 1860

Menemsha. An old Native American word freely translated as "place where demented aliens gather to applaud the setting of the sun while eating supper in the sand."

—ARNIE REISMAN,
in *On the Vineyard II*, 1990

"You come from Cape Cod?" I queried.

"Not far from there," he answered matter-of-factly. "Born and brought up in Falmouth."

—WALTER S. HINCHMAN,
writing as "The Pedestrian," 1920s

When Ephraim Bailey's wedding day came round, it rained, and Ephraim didn't show up at the church. . . . He said, "It rained so hard, I didn't think they'd hold it."

—*WPA Guide to Rhode Island*, 1937

83

[During our hunting season] there's a lot of noise, and now and then we hear a bullet slap into the clapboards, and once in a while we have to stop husking corn and go up in the woods and bring out a wounded hunter. Bringing out a wounded hunter wouldn't be so bad if you didn't have to listen to his comanion explain how he looked like a deer.

—JOHN GOULD,
Neither Hay nor Grass, 1951

Question: How can you tell the recession has hit Rhode Island hard?
Answer: The Mob had to lay off six judges.

—JAMES DODSON,
"The Battle for the Soul of Rhode Island,"
Yankee magazine, 1993

The original Indian name for Connecticut was QUANEH-TA-CUT. The whites have changed the spelling, but it still sounds just as much like a hen's peon of victory after having laid an egg as it ever did.

—WILL M. CRESSEY,
   "The History of Connecticut," 1920s

And tall tales they are! There was the man who shot five bears with one bullet, the man who shot one bear for each day in the year, the man who invented the slow bullet, and the man who fashioned a curved rifle-barrel so efficient that when he shot from his door he had to pull in his head to escape the bullet coming around the house.

—*WPA Maine: A Guide "Down East,"* 1937

The
Educated Yankee

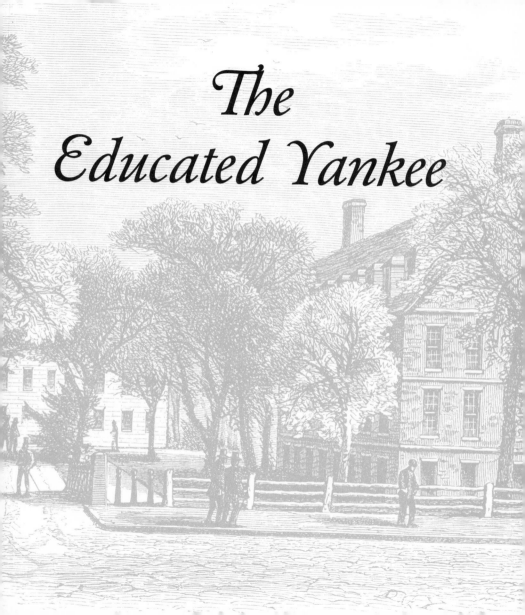

NEW ENGLAND IS KNOWN for its secondary schools and colleges—older and more prestigious than in any other region. Or at least New Englanders like to think so. Pride spills over into snobbery and a kind of starchiness for which New Englanders are also known. The infamous rivalry of Harvard and Yale may seem silly to those outside but it is a deadly serious matter. The educated Yankee is a prideful one, some would say for good reason.

The really important difference between Harvard men and other men is that the former went to Harvard and the latter did not.

—WILLIAM BENTINCK SMITH,
Harvard, 1937

It might be said now that I have the best of both worlds: a Harvard education and a Yale degree.

—JOHN FITZGERALD KENNEDY,
Yale Commencement Address, June 11 1962

The average parent may, for example, plant an artist or fertilize a ballet dancer and end up with a certified public accountant. We cannot train children along chicken wire to make them grow in the right direction. Tying them to stakes is frowned upon, even in Massachusetts.

—ELLEN GOODMAN,
Close to Home, 1979

I don't know why, but I think of all Harvard men as sissies and all Yale men as wearing big blue sweaters and smoking pipes.

—F. SCOTT FITZGERALD,
This Side of Paradise, 1920

Some have said that the [Connecticut] valley is the most educated on the continent. Yale started at its mouth; and Wesleyan remains near the river, as do Trinity and the University of Hartford and Smith and Amherst and Mount Holyoke and the University of Massachusetts and Deerfield Academy and Hampshire College and American International College at Springfield and then further north, Dartmouth College.

—EVAN HILL,
The Connecticut River, 1972

It is, Sir, as I have said, a small college. And yet, there are those who love it!

—DANIEL WEBSTER,
speaking of Dartmouth College,
March 10, 1818

Born to Harvard, she had gone to Smith and returned to marry Harvard. She had grown up in contact with the beauty and the chivalry of Cambridge. She, and presumably her husband as well, represented the cultivation, good manners, consideration for others, cleanliness of body and brightness of mind and dedication to high thinking that were the goals of outsiders like me, dazzled western barbarians aspiring to Rome.

—WALLACE STEGNER,
Crossing to Safety, 1987

The Yale president must be a Yale man. Not too far to the right, too far to the left or a middle-of-the-roader. Ready to give the ultimate word on every subject under the sun from how to handle the Russians to why undergraduates riot in the spring. Profound with a wit that bubbles up and brims over in a cascade of brilliance. You may have guessed who the leading candidate is, but there is a question about him: Is God a Yale man?

—WILMARTH S. LEWIS,
Selections Committee, Yale, 1950

Most literature on the culture of adolescence focuses on peer pressure as a negative force. Warnings about the "wrong crowd" read like tornado alerts in parent manuals. . . . It is a relative term that means different things in different places. In Fort Wayne, for example, the wrong crowd meant hanging out with liberal Democrats. In Connecticut, it meant kids who weren't planning to get a Ph.D. from Yale.

—MARY KAY BLAKELY,
American Mom, 1994

The infant [Amherst] college is an Infant Hercules. Never was so much striving, outstretching, & advancing in a literary cause as is exhibited here.

—RALPH WALDO EMERSON, 1823

If all the girls attending it were laid end to end, [I] wouldn't be at all surprised.

—DOROTHY PARKER,
on the Yale prom, cited in Alexander Woolcott, *While Rome Burns*, 1934

[As a Yale freshman, Calvin] Trillin showed up in New Haven in awe. "People looked like they had costumes on—tweedy sports coats, patches on the elbows. I'd never seen things like that." And of course, he saw men's costumes because the faculty was certainly a male bastion and so was the student body. In those days, Yale was not a study in diversity.

—LARY BLOOM,
"A Yale Education," *Northeast* magazine
of the *Hartford Courant,* March *22, 1998*

Devon is sometimes considered the most beautiful school in New England. . . . It is the beauty of small areas of order—a large yard, a group of trees, three similar dormitories, a circle of old houses—living together in contentious harmony.

—JOHN KNOWLES,
A Separate Peace, 1959

You can always tell a Harvard man, but you can't tell him much.

—ANONYMOUS

When Harvard men say they've graduated from Radcliffe, then we've made it.

—JACQUELINE KENNEDY ONASSIS

Boy, I hated MIT. I worked my butt off for four long years. The only thing that saved my sanity was the 5:15 Club, named, I guess, for the guys who didn't live on campus and took the 5:15 train back home. Yeah, right—5:15, my tush! I never got home before midnight!

—TOM MAGLIOZZI,
cohost of *Car Talk,* from his "auto" biography at Cartalk.cars.com

For the education and instruction of Youth of the Indian Tribes in this Land . . . and also of English Youth and any others.

—Royal charter establishing Dartmouth College, 1769

Gentlemen, you are about to play football for Yale against Harvard. Never in your lives will you ever do anything as important.

—T.A.D. JONES,
Yale football coach, 1920

HARVARD BEATS YALE, 29–29

—Headline in the *Harvard Crimson,*
after Harvard scored 16 points in the last 33 seconds
of the 1968 football game

The
New England
Landscape

THE LANDSCAPE ALONE has done much to forge the character of the people of New England. Steep, rocky hillsides where plows bent and cattle foundered were only some of the challenges presented to the early farmers. The ubiquitous stone walls remind us of the labors of our forebears. The landscape is also the sea and the islands, the lakes and the forests. These natural riches have given rise to literary classics, sprouting poems from the soil.

New England has had a long history, not only in relation to the nation of which she is part, but also in relation to the history of the planet. The folded and faulted rocks that form her bony structure are so ancient that their exact history has not yet been fully deciphered; but most of us know them at least vaguely as examples of "old-worn-down-mountains" in contrast to the "young-rugged-mountains" of the West. The marks of the last wave of glacial ice, on the other hand, are clear and fresh, and lie about us everywhere. Once one learns to see them, the glacier seems a very real and tangible thing, and the twelve thousand years since the ice disappeared become as the twinkling of an eye.

— BETTY FLANDERS THOMSON,
The Changing Face of New England, 1977

Under its shifting sands, the Great Beach hides the wrecks of a hundred ships or more, the debris of civilization.

—JOHN HAY,
"Stranded," *Orion* magazine, Autumn 1992

The village viewed from the top of a hill to the westward, at sunset, has a peculiarly happy and peaceful look; it lies on a level, surrounded by hills, and seems as if it lay in the hollow of a large hand. . . . It is amusing to see all the distributed property, the aristocracy and commonality, the various and conflicting interests of the town, the loves and hates, compressed into a space which the eye takes in as completely as the arrangement of a tea-table.

—NATHANIEL HAWTHORNE,
  on North Adams, Mass.,
  The American Notebooks, 1838

If you were going to be a farmer, you could hardly choose a worse place than New England. (Well, the middle of Lake Erie maybe, but you know what I mean.) the soil is rocky, the terrain steep, and the weather so bad that people take actual pride in it.

—BILL BRYSON,
  A Walk in the Woods, 1998

Provincetown aspires to the condition of Venice. It'll never make it, except maybe in smells.

—ROGER SKILLINGS,
P'town Stories (or The Meatrack), 1980

When Daddy's downcellah busy with his lathe, I go to the edge of our grass to get a look at the Beans. The Beans' mobile home is one of them old ones, looks like a turquoise-blue submarine. It's got blackberry bushes growin' over the windows.

—CAROLYN CHUTE,
The Beans of Egypt, Maine, 1985

If you were going to be a farmer, you could hardly choose a worse place than New England. (Well, the middle of Lake Erie maybe, but you know what I mean.) The soil is rocky, the terrain steep, and the weather so bad that people take actual pride in it.

—BILL BRYSON,
A Walk in the Woods, 1998

Walden Pond was clear and beautiful as usual. It tempted me to bathe; and though the water was thrillingly cold, it was like the thrill of a happy death.

—NATHANIEL HAWTHORNE,
The American Notebooks, 1843

It is a road rich in the effluvia of clams in batter, frying doughnuts, sizzling lard; in tawdriness, cheapness, and bad taste, but in little else.

—KENNETH ROBERTS,
on the highway between Kittery and Portland, Maine,
For Authors Only, 1935

New Hampshire is one big forest.

—BILL BRYSON,
A Walk in the Woods, 1998

Mount Monadnock is to New England what Mount Olympus was to the ancient Mediterranean: not the highest or the grandest mountain, not the wildest or the most difficult, but somehow the most sovereign mountain. It is middle-sized at 3,165 feet and stands alone in the middle of a plain in southern New Hampshire like a clipper ship in a parking lot.

—CASTLE FREEMAN, JR.,
The Old Farmer's Almanac, 1991

There are bogs and bogs but none to equal a Kennebec spruce swamp. Whoever has walked in one will find the hot asphalt of Tophet a pleasant lawn.

—ROBERT P. TRISTRAM COFFIN,
Kennebec, 1937

It looked like the set for an Andy Hardy movie—things quaint in the manner of Norman Rockwell. A small green encircled by Georgian and Federal houses with white picket fences and hitching posts joined the town center of two- and three-story granite buildings, each with many muntined windows. Around the green, along the pickets, lilacs and apple trees blossomed. Maybe the town wasn't the prettiest village in America, but if the townspeople wanted to make that claim, I wouldn't have disputed them. It was Woodstock, Vermont.

—WILLIAM LEAST HEAT-MOON,
Blue Highways, 1982

Later, as I was getting dressed, I'd watch the early sunlight whitewashing the houses across the harbor; America's first light falls on Maine each morning, and a clear and lovely light it is.

—CHARLES KURALT,
America, 1995

Although it can be violent and fierce in a gale, or inscrutable and even threatening when shrouded in fog, the familiar countenance of Cape Cod is gentle and moderate, even touchingly vulnerable, like a set of cherished features deteriorating in the rain of time.

—ROBERT FINCH,
The Cape Itself, 1991

For more than a century, the big business of Gravesend was lumber, which was the first big business of New Hampshire. Although New Hampshire is called the Granite State, granite—building granite, curbstone granite, tombstone granite—came after lumber; it was never the booming business that lumber was. You can be sure that when all the trees are gone, there will still be rocks around; but in the case of granite, most of it remains underground.

—JOHN IRVING,
A Prayer for Owen Meany, 1989

Between Amherst and the Connecticut River lies a little bit of Iowa —some of New England's more favored farmland. The summer and fall of 1982, Judith bicycled, alone and with Jonathan, down narrow roads between fields of asparagus and corn, and she saw the constructed landscape with new eyes, not just looking at houses but searching for ones that might serve as models for her own. She liked the old farmhouses best, their porches and white, clapboarded walls. "This New England farmhousey thing," she called that style.

> —TRACY KIDDER,
> *House,* 1985

Not infrequently this almost landlocked bowl of the heavenliest light you ever experienced, in its thousand shifting nuances from day to night and night to day, scowl to smile, season to season, has been compared with the Bay of Naples alone. And many the traveler has rounded the world, only to return, gaze about him, breathe a deep sigh, and announce as if he had the tablets in hand at last that there was nowhere, anywhere, for that interplay of land and sea and sky and inhabitants to surpass, the old, old fishing port of Gloucester, on the North Shore of Massachusetts Bay.

> —JOSEPH E. GARLAND,
> *The North Shore,* 1998

This is New Hampshire . . . exactly as the Indian gods planted her: raw, beautiful, strong.

—THEODORE VRETTOS,
"Indian Summer," in
New England: The Four Seasons, 1980

A headland of hills of sand, overgrown with scrubby pines, hurts {huckleberries} and such trash, but an excellent harbor for all weathers.

—CAPTAIN JOHN SMITH,
writing about Cape Cod, 1614

The Irishmen soon found they had exchanged the English landlord for the Yankee mill owner; and they took off their hats, these shanty Irish, as reluctantly to this one as they had to the other. As time went on, the shanties disappeared, but the shanty Irishmen remained, housed now in the long row of red-brick tenements put up by the Yankee mill owners.

—MARY DOYLE CURRAN,
The Parish and the Hill, 1948

From sea beach to mountain top all beautiful! Who does not know her fame for wealth, rest, and joy! Her head is in the snows and her feet on the ocean marge. She reaches her hands to all the weary children of men. With her is the delight that does not stale.

—WALLACE NUTTING,
New Hampshire Beautiful, 1923

Life, [my mother] felt, should be everywhere as it was in Amherst, where poverty was an accident and great fortunes unknown. We lived so far from industry that we didn't know the industrial revolution had happened. Yet within a few miles of us were the manufacturing towns of Holyoke, Chicopee and Springfield.

—MARY HEATON VORSE,
A Footnote to Folly, 1935

Welcome to Maine
The way life should be

—Slogan, state of Maine

108

Yankees traditionally build porches that will sag after a decade, and tack them on houses built to stand a century. I think it is a custom smiled upon by church fathers, because it insures that the porch will be a barometer of the morale of whatever occupants may be therein. . . . New England is a harsh climate not only for crops but for neighbors and porches as well. Any flagging of morale—any passing of days skulking indoors in a state of depression . . . any slacking of righteousness—and down goes the porch.

—MARK KRAMER,
Three Farms, 1980

Overnight the brick town of Lowell rose on the Merrimack River, attracting hundreds of farmer's daughters with relatively high wages. For a generation the Lowell factory girls, with their neat dresses, proud deportment and literary weekly, were one of the wonders of America—the first which Charles Dickens, arriving in New England, requested to see.

—CHRISTINA TREE,
How New England Happened, 1976

109

Holyoke is pure New England mill town. . . . First there is the river, wide and full of rapids, swinging around a curve, and then the city itself, climbing the hills on the far bank. Holyoke is vast, dense, and somber. . . . Smokestacks and church spires reach into the sky. There are bricks, millions and millions of dark, sooty bricks, and a wealth of detail: granite windowsills, brass weathervanes, copper-sheathed cupolas, bell towers, ornamental ironwork, heavy wooden doors, cobblestone alleys, stone steps worn smooth by mill-workers' feet.

—BEN BACHMAN,
Upstream, 1985

How high the hill might be, I know not; for, different accounts make it 8, 12 & 16 hundred feet from the river. The prospect repays the ascent and although the day was hot & hazy so as to preclude a distant prospect, yet all the broad meadows in the immediate vicinity of the mountain through which the Connecticut winds, make a beautiful picture seldom rivalled.

—RALPH WALDO EMERSON,
on Mount Holyoke in Massachusetts, 1823

[From] the eastern brow of the mountain . . . we had a view over the tops of a multitude of heights, into the intersecting vallies of which we were to plunge—and beyond them the blue and indistinctive scene extended, to the east and north, to the distance of at least sixty miles. Beyond the hills, it looked almost as if the blue ocean might be seen. Monadnock was visible, like a blue cloud against the sky

—NATHANIEL HAWTHORNE,
The American Notebooks, 1838

The river was a brawling stream, shallow, and roughened by rocks; now we rode on a level with it; now there was a sheer descent down from the roadside upon it. . . . Between the mountains there were gorges and defiles, that led the imagination away into new scenes of wildness. I have never ridden through such romantic scenery.

—NATHANIEL HAWTHORNE,
on the Deerfield River,
The American Notebooks, 1838

III

[My] route . . . brings me down and around to the city proper, a long, straight street in another country, with homemade shop signs in Spanish, blocks of Third World decay, citizens of many colors draped in windows, doorways, on corners, in parked cars, often with a look in their eyes that asks what you're asking—Is this the right place, how in the hell did I wind up here?

—JOHN EDGAR WIDEMAN,
on Springfield, Mass., *Fartheralong,* 1994

The time must come when this coast will be a place of resort for those New-Englanders who really wish to visit the seaside. . . . If it is merely a ten-pin alley, or a circular railway, or an ocean of mint-julep that the visitor is in search of . . . I trust that for a long time, he will be disappointed here.

—HENRY DAVID THOREAU,
Cape Cod, 1865

112

It is a wonder that Norwood was ever allowed to venture so near to the low grounds of the Connecticut; for it was early settled, not far from thirty years after the Pilgrims' landing. How the temptation to build upon the top of the highest hill was resisted, we know not.

>—HENRY WARD BEECHER,
> on Northampton ("Norwood"), Mass., *Norwood; Or,*
> *Village Life in New England,* 1868

In September and October one never walks or drives through this Connecticut Valley without smiling at these ungainly mounds of squashes and pumpkins heaped in uneven, bulging pyramids on green grass, or against barnyard fences, or under bright trees, or before the doors of farmhouses.

>—MARY ELLEN CHASE,
> *A Journey to Boston,* 1965

In front of me stretched the water of Quabbin. It was for this water that the Swift River Valley was flooded. It was because of this water that the wilderness, with its eagles and its extensive woodlands and abandoned cellar holes, exists in the Quabbin region.

—THOMAS CONUEL,
Quabbin: The Accidental Wilderness, 1981

The weather-beaten granite has an individuality which belongs to this corner of the land and marks it as a stone fit for our builder's purposes. Under every sort of weather—and we have them all in Connecticut—it throws back the light in a warm and friendly glow. Its texture is as rough as homespun, its strength as rugged as the pioneer's; yet in the late afternoon, its surface seems to grow softer and more mellow, under the slanting rays of the sun, much as a face that is usually a little stern and rigid may melt into more genial lines under the influence of friendship. The character of New England is stamped upon this stone.

—ROBERT DUDLEY FRENCH, 1929

In Vermont no back road of any pride is content to have only one name. In the next town to me and its neighbors to the north, for example, Grassy Brook Road becomes Archie Jones Road, becomes Lower Road, becomes Route 35, becomes Weaver Brook Road, becomes Cambridgeport Road—all in the course of about 15 miles of the same thoroughfare.

—CASTLE FREEMAN, JR.,
"Unimproved Roads," *Yankee* magazine, March 1998

When I was growing up, in the 1950s, my grandparents had a farm outside Hartford, [on] one of the four corners of a crossroads. The farm was surrounded by orchards, and there was a skating pond for the winter and blueberry bushes for July and August picking. By the time I was a teenager, the three other corners were being filled in, and there were supermarkets and gas stations standing on old farmland. By the time I got out of college, my grandparents' farm had become a regional shopping mall.

—ROBERT YARO, quoted in
The Experience of Place by Tony Hiss, 1990

Today the human footprint is all over the place. The old salts and first families are only dimly evident, towns are run by business interests. . . . No one even considers the possibility of keeping the Island as it was. Instead they debate the ideal rate of growth.

—ANNE W. SIMON,
On the Vineyard II, 1990

You claim New England's a pretty place? Think again. Oh, it's fine for hiking or camping; it's got all those swell bubbling brooks; it's peaceful and clean and colorful. But, look, when it comes to something truly *important*, like the game of golf, these northeastern states can be downright grotesque.

—TIM O'BRIEN,
"The Beholder's Eye," in
New England: The Four Seasons, 1980

116

A town is not land, nor even landscape. A town is people living on the land. And whether it will survive or perish depends not on the land but on the people; it depends on what the people think they are. . . . If they think of themselves as living a good and useful and satisfying life, if they put their lives first and the real estate business after, then there is nothing inevitable about the spreading ruin of the countryside.

> —ARCHIBALD MACLEISH,
> "A Lay Sermon on Hill Towns," 1978

A great ocean beach runs north and south unbroken, mile lengthening into mile. Solitary and elemental, unsullied and remote, visited and possessed by the outer sea, these sands might be the end or the beginning of the world.

> —HENRY BESTON,
> *The Outermost House*, 1928

Instead of fences, the earth was sometimes thrown up into a slight ridge. My companion compared it to the rolling prairies of Illinois. In the storm of wind and rain which raged when we traversed it, it no doubt appeared more vast and desolate than it really is. . . . A solitary traveller whom we saw perambulating in the distance loomed like a giant. . . . Indeed, to an inlander, the Cape landscape is a constant mirage.

—HENRY DAVID THOREAU,
Cape Cod, 1865

You come up here on a fine afternoon and you can see range on range of hills—awful blue they are—up there by Lake Sunapee and Lake Winnipesaukee . . . and way up, if you've got a glass, you can see the White Mountains and Mt. Washington—where North Conway and Conway is. And, of course, our favorite mountain, Mt. Monadnock's right there—and all these towns that lie around it: Jaffrey and East Jaffrey, and Peterborough, and Dublin; and there, quite a ways down, is Grover's Corners.

—THORNTON WILDER,
Our Town, 1938

There's something soft about Cape Cod that doesn't appeal to me
too much. But there's a beautiful light there—very luminous—
perhaps because it's so far out to sea; an island almost.

—EDWARD HOPPER,
    cited in *The Artist's Voice,* 1962

This is big country, larger than Connecticut and Rhode Island combined, nearly the equal of Massachusetts; its vastness is more sug-
gestive of the West than of New England. Its winters, people will
tell you, are fiercer, its forests thicker, its rivers wilder than anywhere else in the East.

—MEL ALLEN,
    on Aroostook County, Maine,
    in "There's No Easy Way to Pick Potatoes,"
    Yankee magazine, September 1978

Maine lakes may still be observed during moments of soundlessness—in the pure luxury of quiet. Yet for those who long to hear those rare sounds once more, there is always the hope that there will be loons calling—breaking the silence with their wild arousing cries.

—LEE KINGMAN,
"Meditation in Maine,"
in *New England: The Four Seasons, 1980*

This stream may perhaps with more propriety than any other in the world be named the beautiful river. From Stuart to the Sound it uniformly maintains this character. The purity, salubrity and sweetness of its waters; the frequency and elegance of its meanders; its absolute freedom from all aquatic vegetables; the uncommon and universal beauty of its banks, here a smooth and winding beach, there covered with rich verdure, now fringed with bushes, now covered with lofty trees, and now formed by the intruding hill, the rude bluff and the shaggy mountain—are objects which no traveler can thoroughly describe.

—TIMOTHY DWIGHT,
on the Connecticut River, early 1800s

[New England villages] are one of the great sights of the western world—red buildings to house the cattle, white ones to hold the spirit, and trees like the spirit itself abroad on the countryside.

—JANE LANGTON,
"New England Classic,"
in *New England: The Four Seasons,* 1980

It was another Vermont house, white, of course, with long and narrow windows like New England faces.

—JOHN KNOWLES,
A Separate Peace, 1959

[The] idea, of land held in common, as . . . part of a manifest, workaday covenant with the Bestower of a new continent, has permanently imprinted the maps of these towns, and lengthens the perspectives of those who live within them.

—JOHN UPDIKE,
"Common Land,"
in *New England: The Four Seasons,* 1980

To the entire world, a steepled church, set in its frame of white wooden homes around a manicured common, remains a scene which says "New England."

—CHRISTINA TREE,
How New England Happened, 1976

I hung over the Concord River then as long as I could, and recalled how Thoreau, Hawthorne, Emerson himself, have expressed with due sympathy the sense of this full, slow, sleepy meadowy flood, which sets its pace and takes its twists like some large obese benevolent person, scarce so frankly unsociable as to pass you at all. . . . [It] draws along the woods and the orchards and the fields with the purr of a mild domesticated cat who rubs against the family and furniture.

—HENRY JAMES,
The American Scene, 1907

Warren is the smallest town in the smallest county in . . . Rhode Island, a state that every schoolchild learns is no larger than a postage stamp.

—BOB WYSS,
"Warren, Rhode Island," *Yankee* magazine, August 1984

122

They have covered a bare and uncouth cluster of gray ledges with houses, and called it Marblehead. These ledges stick out everywhere; there is not enough soil to cover them decently. The original gullies intersecting these ledges were turned into thoroughfares, which meander about after a most lawless and inscrutable fashion. . . .We expect to see sailors in pigtails, citizens in periwigs, and women in kerchiefs and hobnail shoes, all speaking an unintelligible jargon.

—SAMUEL DRAKE,
on Marblehead, Mass., *A Book of New England Legends and Folk Lore,* 1872

[If] the river is as varied and beautiful as the Connecticut, you can merely look at it—in the long light of a sultry summer evening, under an angry winter sky, in the high color of autumn or the pastel shades of spring—and derive that sense of peace and uplift of the spirit that most men find in living water.

—ROGER TORY PETERSON,
in *The Connecticut River* by Evan Hill, 1972

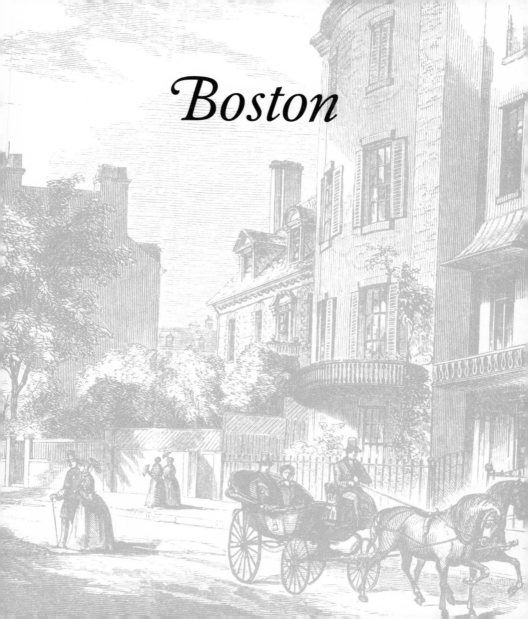

Boston

IF THE STATE HOUSE IN BOSTON is the hub of the solar system, as Oliver Wendell Holmes claimed, then surely Boston is the hub of New England. A modest city with a great history and definite parameters, Boston is like none other in America. Its peculiarities, such as its lack of signs and difficulty of in driving anywhere, have made it the butt of many jokes. The World Series woes of the Red Sox and sports angst, in general, seem to single it out as a delicate city, defensive and easily hurt. The relative lack of nightlife makes it seem genteel and mannered, an old uncle we love to visit whose somewhat eccentric rules we must live by so long as we are under his roof. Boston, oh, Boston!

Reduced to simplest terms, New England consists of two regions: Boston and Not-Boston.

—WAYNE CURTIS,
Frommer's 2001 New England

Boston is a good town to write in—perhaps the best, just as New York is the best town to live in.

—EDWARD ARLINGTON ROBINSON (1869–1935)

[In] New York, the women walk as though in the rain; in Boston, many women stroll.

—ANDRE DUBUS,
Broken Vessels, 1991

Boston is a good place to live in, taken all in all. Probably the bes
place in this neurotic world, with the possible exception of Londo
although I am not even sure about this. At any rate, it is the only
place I care to live in.

—JOHN P. MARQUAND,
The Late George Apley, 1937

Criticizing Boston's taxicabs is about as controversial as taking a
stand against earthquakes, ax murderers, or the Third Reich. . . .The
drivers themselves are generally friendly but often topographically
confused. . . No two rides are the same. No two taxis take you from
Point A to Point B via Route C. And even if they do, the fares are
somehow different. To enter a taxi in the Hub is to embark on a
magical mystery tour of assorted mechanical surprises and geograph-
ic wonders.

—NATHAN COBB,
"Taxiing Toward a Fun City,"
in *Cityside/Countryside,* 1980

In my Aunt Martha's day, to grow up in Gravesend was to understand that Boston was a city of sin. And even though my mother
had stayed in a highly approved and chaperoned women's residential
hotel, she had managed to have her "fling," as Aunt Martha called
it, with [a] man she'd met on the Boston & Maine.

—JOHN IRVING,
A Prayer for Owen Meany, 1989

For serious looking at baseball there are few places better than
Fenway Park. The stands are close to the playing field, the fences are
a hopeful green and the young men in their white uniforms are
working on real grass, the authentic natural article; under the actual
sky in the temperature as it really is. No Tartan Turf. No Astrodome.
No air conditioning. Not too many pennants over the years, but no
Texans either.

—ROBERT B. PARKER,
Mortal Stakes, 1975

It's a well-known fact, at least in northern New England, that the enthusiasm of Red Sox fans tends to increase in direct proportion to their distance from Fenway Park.

—HOWARD FRANK MOSHER,
A Stranger in the Kingdom, 1989

Boston State-house is the hub of the solar system.

—OLIVER WENDELL HOLMES,
The Autocrat of the Breakfast-Table, 1858

There is no section in America half so good to live in as splendid old New England —& there is no city on this continent so lovely & loveable as Boston.

—MARK TWAIN,
in a letter to Mollie Clemens,
January 1871

In Boston there is an utter absence of that wild electric beauty of New York, of the marvelous, excited rush of people in taxicabs at twilight, of the great Avenues and Streets, the restaurants, theatres, bars, hotels, delicatessens, shops. In Boston the night comes down with an incredibly heavy, small-town finality. The cows come home; the chickens go to roost; the meadow is dark. Nearly every Bostonian is in his house or in someone else's house, dining at the home board, enjoying domestic and social privacy.

—ELIZABETH HARDWICK,
Harper's Magazine, December 1959

Boston is a curious place. . . . When a society has reached this point, it acquires a self-complacency which is wildly exasperating. My fingers itch to puncture it; to do something which will sting it into impropriety.

—HENRY ADAMS,
letter of 1875

There broods over the real Boston an immense effect of finality. One feels in Boston, as one feels in no other part of the States, that the intellectual movement has ceased.

—H. G. WELLS,
The Future in America, 1906

I care a great deal to prevent myself from becoming what of all things I despise, a Boston prig. . . . Anything which takes a man morally out of Beacon Street, Nahant and Beverly Farms, Harvard College and the Boston press, must be in itself a good.

—HENRY ADAMS,
letter of 1875

I guess God made Boston on a wet Sunday.

—RAYMOND CHANDLER
letter of March 21, 1949

Boston runs to brains as well as to beans and brown bread. But she is cursed with an army of cranks whom nothing short of a straitjacket or a swamp elm club will ever control.

—WILLIAM COWPER BRANN,
The Iconoclast, Texas newspaper published in the 1890s

We say the cows laid out Boston. Well, there are worse surveyors.

—RALPH WALDO EMERSON,
"Wealth," 1860

Generations of mariners have testified to the ocean's bounty—in the "Sacred Cod," that marvelous and deceptively simple carving that hangs in Boston's State House.

—*American Heritage Book of Great Historic Places,* 1957

Fenway Park, in Boston, is a lyric little bandbox of a ballpark. Everything is painted green and seems in curiously sharp focus, like the inside of an old fashioned peeping-type Easter egg.

—JOHN UPDIKE
"Hub Fans Bid Kid Adieu,"
New Yorker, October 22, 1960

Not a player on the field and not a Sox fan watching on television emerged unscathed from the devastating loss to the Mets. None would escape the feeling of watching the ball bounce between Bill Buckner's legs.

—GLENN STOUT AND RICHARD A. JOHNSON,
Red Sox Century, 2000

It is said that the spectators at Boston will not let you drop out, they just push you back on the course.

> —JOHN PRIESTER,
> after the 2002 Boston Marathon

Some want to rob the Puritans of art. . . . There were ten silversmiths in Boston before there was a single lawyer. People forget all those things.

> —ROBERT FROST,
> *"What Became of New England?"* Commencement Address at Oberlin College, 1937

A huckleberry never reaches Boston; they have not been known there since they grew on her three hills.

—HENRY DAVID THOREAU,
Walden, 1845

The high-ceilinged rooms, the little balconies, alcoves, nooks and angles all suggest sanctuary, escape, creature comfort. The reader, the scholar, the browser, the borrower is king.

—DAVID MCCORD:
On the Boston Athenaeum, *Time,* November 15, 1982

It's in that section of Boston, isn't it? Then call it Fenway Park.

—JOHN I. TAYLOR,
Red Sox owner, 1912

This can be a cold place, Boston, and the weather is the least of it. We're often unwelcoming to outsiders. We have a maddening trait of sniping at insiders. We have equal parts determination and aloofness proudly bred into our native bones like the hunting instincts in a championship dog.

—BRIAN MCGRORY,
The Boston Globe, March 15, 2002

America, the new world, compares in glamour and romance with the old, and Boston Harbor is one of the most delightful places in America.

—EDWARD ROWE SNOW,
The Islands of Boston Harbor, 1935

Boston is a moral and intellectual nursery, always applying first
principles to trifles.

—GEORGE SANTAYANA (1863–1952)

The old Boston Garden seats, some of which are placed here, were,
as we remembered not much fun to sit in. The museum displays a
sense of humor, by placing one seat behind a pole, symbolizing the
1,895 such seats.

—JIM SULLIVAN,
on the Sports Museum of New England, *'Take Me Out To,"
Boston Globe,* April 11, 2002

And this is good old Boston,
The home of the bean and the cod,
Where the Lowells talk to the Cabots
And the Cabots talk only to God.

—JOHN COLLINS BOSSIDY,
Holy Cross alumni dinner, 1910

In Boston they ask, How much does he know? In New York, How much is he worth? In Philadelphia, Who were his parents?

—MARK TWAIN,
  "What Paul Bourget Thinks of Us," 1895

It used to be said that, socially speaking, Philadelphia asked who a person is, New York how much is he worth, and Boston what does he know. Nationally it has now become generally recognized that Boston Society has long cared even more than Philadelphia about the first point and has refined the asking of who a person is to the point of demanding to know who he was. Philadelphia asks about a man's parents; Boston wants to know about his grandparents.

—CLEVELAND AMORY,
  The Proper Bostonians, 1947

A town that boasts inhabitants like me
Can have no lack of good society.

—HENRY WADSWORTH LONGFELLOW,
"The Poets Tale; The Birds of Killgworth,"
Tales of a Wayside Inn, 1863

The humblest man of letters has a position here which he doesn't have in New York. To be known as an able writer is to have the choicest society open to you. . . . A knight of the quill here is supposed necessarily to be a gentleman. In New York—he's a Bohemian!

—THOMAS BAILEY ALDRICH,
on Boston, quoted in *New England Summer*
by Van Wyck Brooks, 1940

In Boston they understand each other with very few words said.

—OWEN WISTER,
Rude Britannia, Crude Columbia, A Straight Deal, or The Ancient Grudge, 1920

From *Harper's Bazaar,* which is my Bible, I learn that the Boston group in North Haven frown on new garments in their summer colony, and that a man in a new pair of sneakers is snubbed. "The older the clothes, the bluer the blood," says the writer. . . . I am aging a pair of sneakers and a jacket in case I should meet a Bostonian in warm weather.

—E. B. WHITE,
One Man's Meat, 1944

I have just returned from Boston. It is the only sane thing to do if you find yourself up there.

—FRED ALLEN,
in a letter to Groucho Marx, June 12, 1953

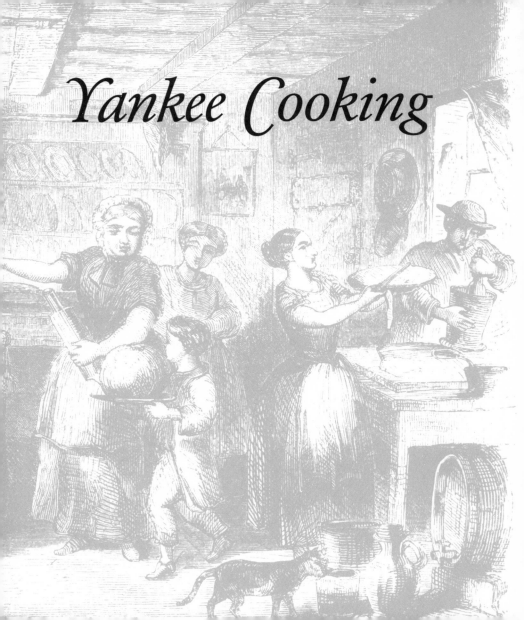

Yankee Cooking

Do we love it or hate it? Does anyone ever eat a fish ball nowadays? Perhaps not but bean suppers continue to prevail in the outer regions of the province. New England culinary classics are part of the culture; hearty, starchy, simple to create, they are, like many other things, vanishing into the proliferation of chain restaurants and fast food emporiums. But the essence of the meal—the red flannel hash, the boiled dinner, the steamed lobster, the baked beans, the apple pandowdy—all of it is and will be forever a flag which any Yankee will salute.

For breakfast, the baked beans again—warmed over, of course—and fish balls. I don't remember ever having fish balls on Saturday, but we never failed to have them Sunday morning. Sometimes rye-meal muffins instead of the brown bread, but beans and fish balls, always. A solid orthodox breakfast like that laid the foundation for the orthodox day that followed.

—JOSEPH C. LINCOLN,
Cape Cod Yesterdays, 1935

The National Doughnut Dunking Association has always credited the invention of its pet provender to a Maine sea captain named Hanson Gregory. . . .[In 1847] objecting to the soggy center in his mother's fried cakes, [he] is said to have remarked, "Why don't you cut a hole in the middle where it doesn't cook?" . . . But now a Cape Cod historian places the event earlier by a good two hundred years. It seems that one day back in the seventeenth century a Nauset Indian playfully shot an arrow through a fried cake his squaw was making. The squaw, frightened, dropped the perforated patty into a kettle of boiling grease—and the result was the doughnut.

—LOUIS P. DE GOUY,
The Gold Cook Book, 1970

145

Aunt Fanny's headstone in the roadside graveyard is moss-stained . . . but her reputation as queen of the kitchen still lingers in the village of Franconia, for she was one of those natural cooks who are "born with a mixing spoon in one hand and a rolling pin in the other." New England has produced many. They invented baked Indian pudding and apple pandowdy. They established the boiled dinner as a Thursday institution, and Boston baked beans and brown bread as the typical Saturday night supper.

—ELLA SHANNON BOWLES and DOROTHY S. TOWLE,
Secrets of New England Cooking, 1947

I ate a grinder—elsewhere called a hero, hoagie, poorboy, submarine, sub, torpedo, Italian—and drank a chocolate frappe—elsewhere called a milkshake or malted. Although the true milkshake doesn't exist east of the Appalachians, the grinder was the best thing to happen to me in a day: thinly sliced beef and ham, slivered tomatoes, chopped lettuce, and minced hot peppers, all dressed down with vinegar and oil. I went back to the window to order another.

—WILLIAM LEAST HEAT MOON,
Blue Highways, 1982

146

Fieldmouse Pie

5 fat field mice
1 cup macaroni
1/2 medium onion, thinly sliced
1 medium-size can tomatoes
1 cup cracker crumbs

Boil the macaroni 10 minutes. While it is cooking, fry field mice long enough to fry out excess fat. Grease casserole with some of the fat and put a layer of macaroni in it. Add onion and tomatoes, then salt and pepper it well. Add field mice and cover with the remaining macaroni. Sprinkle the top with cracker crumbs seasoned with salt, pepper, and butter. Bake at 325 degrees for 20 minutes or until mice are well done. (Note: if insufficient mice are available, substitute sausages.)

—Originally published in a 19th-century cookbook
by a group of ladies from Grafton, Vt.

Everybody remembers the recipe for cooking a coot: put an ax in the pan with the coot, and when you can stick a fork in the ax the coot is done.

—John Gould,
"They Come High," in *New England: The Four Seasons,* 1980

A true Rhode Island Yankee will have jonny-cakes with all three meals: with bacon and eggs in the morning; with pork chops and boiled potatoes at noon; and with Yankee pot roast for supper.

—DONALD J. BOISVERT,
500 Tomato Plants in the Kitchen, 2001

Every New England girl who lived within sound of the sea, four or five generations ago, counted a chowder kettle as an essential part of her "setting out." When a bride left the family homestead, she carried with her a huge iron pot in which to make the hearty dish of fish, swimming in rich broth flavored with salt pork and onions.

—ELLA SHANNON BOWLES and DOROTHY S. TOWLE,
Secrets of New England Cooking, 1947

Alas, what crimes have been committed in the name of chowder! Dainty chintz-draped tea rooms, charity bazaars, church suppers, summer hotels, canning factories—all have shamelessly travestied one of America's noblest institutions; yet while clams and onions last, the chowder shall not die.

—LOUIS P. DE GOUY,
The Gold Cook Book, 1970

Rusks, baked in cake tins, and broken and cut into wedges when served, are as popular today as they were when Lady Pepperell, wife of the hero of Louisburg, served them in the ancient mansion in Kittery, Maine. The same recipe used by the famous eighteenth-century hostess has survived the years. We give it here, with little idea that you will try to make rusks in such quantities: To make rusks, take 1 pd. of flower, 1 pd. of sugar, 3 pints of milk, 20 eggs, half a pint of yeast. The butter and the sugar put into the milk and make it bloodwarm, the eggs and the yeast mix together and work it well, let it rise well, bake it.

—ELLA SHANNON BOWLES and DOROTHY S. TOWLE, *Secrets of New England Cooking,* 1947

The secret to cooking lobsters is not to murder them. Give them a nice respectable way out. Don't put them in boiling water and don't drown them in too much water. . . . I put in two inches of water, whether I'm cooking two lobsters or 14. . . . When the water is boiling, put in the lobsters, put the lid on, and steam them for 20 minutes, not a minute less and not a minute more.

—BERTHA NUNAN, *Yankee* magazine, June 1979

People all over New England, of course, have always baked clams on the beach—built a fire of hardwood over stones that will retain the heat, then piled on four or five inches of rockweed that pops and sizzles as it steams—but the custom seems particularly institutionalized around Providence. . . . Around Narragansett Bay . . . the tradition of clam bakes seems to have outlasted the clams.

—CALVIN TRILLIN,
The Tummy Trilogy, 1994

When I was young in Vermont, there was a fine-looking man who lived across the street from us. His wife told us that in his whole life he had never missed having a piece of pie for breakfast each morning. We looked upon this fortunate creature with an awe that was not unmixed with envy, for the fine old New England breakfast had disappeared already from our table. Oatmeal, ham, creamed codfish, cornbread, . . . yes; pie . . .

—SARA B. B. STAMM,
Favorite New England Recipes, 1972

The aroma [in the farm kitchen] was a combination of wood smoke and hot iron, lingering cookery, drying mittens and socks, warming boots, barn clothes, wintering geraniums on the window sills, and the relaxed effluence of a lazy beagle toasting under the stove.

—JOHN GOULD,
Next Time Around, 1983

[An] ancient wooden shack [stands] among magnificent old maple trees. When we came first in sight of it, it looked as though it were on fire, for the steam from the boiling sap was pouring out through every crack. It was indeed a stirring place—men and boys hallooing in the woods as they chopped fuel for the fire, and drove the sledges down the mountainside with barrels of sap, or ran in and out of the sugarhouse. As we came nearer we caught the ambrosial odor of the steaming syrup.

—RAY STANNARD BAKER
(writing as David Grayson),
The Countryman's Year, 1936

Fiddle ferns, if you know where to find them, are the first delicacy of spring, appearing even before asparagus. Plunge them briefly in rapidly boiling water, and serve with butter, salt, and if you like, lemon juice. Chopped almonds may be added, or the ferns may be served on hot buttered toast.

—SARA B. B. STAMM,
Favorite New England Recipes, 1972

Several score of the best-educated, most agreeable, and personally the most sociable people in America united in Cambridge to make a social dessert that would have starved a polar bear.

—HENRY ADAMS,
The Education of Henry Adams, 1907

Believing it to be the root of all human ills, our forefathers avoided drinking water whenever possible. . . . [In] the early days, family brewing was as important as family baking . . . and every housewife had her favorite recipes.

—ELLA SHANNON BOWLES and DOROTHY S. TOWLE,
Secrets of New England Cooking, 1947

There is a terrible pink mixture (with tomatoes in it, and herbs) called Manhattan Clam Chowder, that is only a vegetable soup, and not to be confused with New England Clam Chowder, nor spoken of in the same breath. Tomatoes and clams have no more affinity than ice cream and horse radish. It is sacrilege to wed bivalves, with bay leaves and only a degraded cook would do such a thing.

—ELEANOR EARLY,
A New England Sampler, 1940

Traditionally the Yankee breakfast has been a fine, warm affair, a minor feast that can hold its own with any other meal. Yankees rose early (most of them still do), and the chores that had to be done while breakfast was prepared produced a happy appetite for fish cakes, baked beans, and pie. The only restriction to dishes that should please a hungry man was that they had to be something kept over from the day before or possible to cook in a reasonably short time.

—SARA B. B. STAMM,
Favorite New England Recipes, 1972

Poems have been written about bouillabaise; but I have tried it again and again in the world's leading bouillabaise centers, and, on the words of a dispassionate reporter, it's not to be compared with a Maine cunner, cod, or haddock chowder made with salt pork and common crackers.

—KENNETH ROBERTS,
Trending into Maine, 1938

No New England garden was considered a success if it did not furnish a large mess of green peas for Fourth of July dinner. If the season were a late one, the whole family watched the rows of peas anxiously. If the season were early, the peas were left on the vine to be sure of enough to go with the fresh salmon and lemon sherbet.

—ELLA SHANNON BOWLES and DOROTHY S. TOWLE,
Secrets of New England Cooking, 1947

154

Today, no summer is really perfect for the New Englander until, napkin under chin, he has eaten his fill of fresh steamed clams, dipped in broth and then in melted butter.

—ELLA SHANNON BOWLES and DOROTHY S. TOWLE,
Secrets of New England Cooking, 1947

She boiled three good-sized potatoes for 25 minutes; then mashed them and stirred the fish into them. To this mixture she added five eggs, five generous teaspoons of butter and a little pepper, beat everything vigorously together. She cooked them in deep fat, picking up generous dabs of the mixture in a potbellied spoon. The resulting fish balls, eaten with her own brand of ketchup, made ambrosia seem like pretty dull stuff.

—KENNETH ROBERTS,
Trending into Maine, 1938

Sense
of Place

PERHAPS NOWHERE ELSE IN THIS COUNTRY is there such a strong sense of place as there is in New England, America's hometown, the place from which we came and to which we long to return. The landscape, the people, the food, the weather and the seasons, all combine to stir allegiance and a strong sense of nostalgia for the way things used to be. New England changes, as do all regions, but nowhere is there such a desire to keep things the way they are, to hold on to the old ways, to preserve and protect and maintain a place so dear to so many, here and abroad.

For more than a hundred years, anybody willing to leave this country-side has been rewarded for leaving it by more money, leisure, and creature comforts. A few may have stayed from fecklessness or lack of gumption; more have stayed from family feeling or homesickness; but most stay from love. I live among a population, extraordinary in our culture, that lives where it lives because it loves its place. We are self-selected place-lovers. There's no reason to live here except for love.

> —DONALD HALL,
> *Seasons at Eagle Pond,* 1987

What are springs and waterfalls? Here is the spring of springs, the waterfall of waterfalls. A storm in the fall or winter is the time to visit it; a light-house or a fisherman's hut the true hotel. A man may stand there and put all America behind him.

> —HENRY DAVID THOREAU,
> *Cape Cod,* 1865

In Vermont, wherever you turn, you drink up beauty like rich milk, and feel its wholesome strength seep into your sinews.

—SARAH N. CLEGHORN,
Threescore: The Autobiography of Sarah N. Cleghorn, 1936

Vermont, Designed by the Creator for the Playground of the Continent.

—First state-sponsored tourist brochure, 1911

I shall enter on no encomium upon Massachusetts; she needs none. There she is. Behold her, and judge for yourselves. There is her history; the world knows it by heart. The past, at least, is secure. There is Boston and Concord and Lexington and Bunker Hill; and there they will remain forever.

—DANIEL WEBSTER,
Second Speech on Foot's Resolution, 1830

Vermont is a state I love. I could not look upon the peaks of Ascutney, Killington and Mansfield without being moved in a way that no other scene could move me. It was here that I first saw the light of day, here that I received my bride. Here my dead lie buried, pillowed among the everlasting hills. I love Vermont because of her hills and valleys, her scenery and invigorating climate, but most of all, I love her because of her indomitable people. They are a race of pioneers who almost impoverished themselves for love of others. If ever the spirit of liberty should vanish from the rest of the Union, it could be restored by the generous share held by the people in this brave little State of Vermont.

—CALVIN COOLIDGE,
extemporaneous remarks from a railroad observation car,
Bennington, Vt., 1928

Vermont is a land filled with milk and maple syrup, and overrun with New Yorkers.

—JOHN L. GARRISON, 1946

161

She's one of the two best states in the Union. Vermont's the other.

—ROBERT FROST,
"New Hampshire," 1923

Today I'd like nothing more strenuous than to sit still and admire the huge heads of phlox that the wet season has produced in the perennial borders and watch the bees sipping nectar from the poisonous monkshood and plundering the lavender spikes of the veronicas. But a gardener's mind is restless; it runs on ahead, and that is the penalty one pays for the life of culture.

—KATHARINE S. WHITE,
Onward and Upward in the Garden, 1979

I have seen rather more of the world's surface than most men ever do, and I have chosen the valley of this river for my home.

—ROGER TORY PETERSON,
in *The Connecticut River* by Evan Hill, 1972

Not only was she traditional by nature, Katharine showed a strong streak of parochialism in her approach to gardening. New England was what she knew as a child, and the roots of her ancestors went deep in the soil of Maine and of Massachusetts. The things that grew in New England, therefore, were "correct." They occupied a special place in her heart, an authenticity not enjoyed by flowers that made the mistake of blooming in other sections of the country.

—E.B. WHITE,
in *Onward and Upward in the Garden*
by Katharine White, 1979

During the years that I lived with my grandparents in Lost Nation Hollow, a number of itinerant specialists could be counted on to visit Kingdom County each year. I had no idea where most of these exotic wayfarers hailed from. "Away," most of us called anywhere more than five miles beyond the county line. Or "the other side of the hills." All I knew for certain is that since we could not go to them, the mind readers and barnstorming four-man baseball teams and one-elephant family circuses came to us.

—HOWARD FRANK MOSHER,
Northern Borders, 1994

Walpole, New Hampshire, is small enough for us to keep that mom-and-pop feeling. The town reminds us every day of the power of history. And it's important to stay in a place where whatever notoriety you get, plus fifty cents, will buy you a cup of coffee.

—KEN BURNS,
"Three Questions, Three Answers,"
Yankee magazine, July/August 2002

As I think about it today in my 81st year, looking out at the sea from my desk, I realize that what I have found in Maine is more than courtesy and kindness. It is grace.

—MAY SARTON,
"I Was on My Way Home Anyway,"
Yankee magazine, March 1994

Vermont is my birthright. People there are happy and content. They belong to themselves, live within their income, and fear no man.

—CALVIN COOLIDGE, 1920

Exile is always difficult, and yet I could not have imagined a better place to live, and wait for my return home, than Cavendish, Vermont.

> —ALEKSANDR SOLZHENITSYN,
>> in a letter to the town of Cavendish upon his return
>> to Russia after ten years in Vermont, 1994

[In Vineyard Haven] I like the whole barefoot, chattering melee on Main Street—even, God help me, the gawking tourists with their Instamatics and their avoirdupois. I like the preposterous gingerbread bank and the local lady shoppers with their Down East accents, discussing *bahgins.*

> —WILLIAM STYRON,
>> "In Praise of Vineyard Haven," in *On the Vineyard II,* 1990

I moved to New England partly because it has a real literary past. The ghosts of Hawthorne and Melville still sit on those green hills. The worship of Mammon is also somewhat lessened there by the spirit of irony. I don't get hay fever in New England either.

> —JOHN UPDIKE,
>> *London Observer*, March 25, 1979

As he looked up and down the long vista, and saw the clear white houses glancing here and there in the broken moonshine, he could almost have believed that the happiest lot for any man was to make the most of life in some such tranquil spot as that. Here were kindness, comfort, safety, the warning voice of duty, the perfect hush of temptation.

—HENRY JAMES,
writing of Northampton, Mass.,
in *Roderick Hudson*, 1875

Single spots, finer than any in New England, there may be in other lands; but such a series of villages over such a breadth of country, amidst so much beauty of scenery, enriched, though with charming and inexpensive simplicity, with so much beauty of garden, yard, and dwelling, cannot elsewhere be found upon the globe.

—HENRY WARD BEECHER,
Norwood; Or, Village Life in New England, 1868

166

Lighthouses, from ancient times, have fascinated and intrigued members of the human race. There is something about a lighted beacon that suggests hope and trust and appeals to the better instincts of mankind.

—EDWARD ROWE SNOW,
Famous Lighthouses of New England, 1945

Perhaps nowhere is the notion of romance more firmly embedded than at the Edgartown Light.

—JULIA WELLS,
"History of Vineyard Lighthouses,"
Vineyard Gazette, April 7, 2001

And of all the foure parts of the world that I have yet seene not inhabited, could I have but meanes to transport a Colonie, I would rather live here than anywhere.

—CAPTAIN JOHN SMITH,
on the Isles of Shoals, 1614

I live right in the heart of New England . . . and I have to say that things are very good here. Just yesterday I walked down Main Street. The soap store, the candle store, the balloon store were all full of customers. The sticker store, too. . . . Brisk business at the Juice Bar, with a new item featured: fresh wheatgrass juice.

—RICHARD TODD,
  "Notes from the Transcendental Valley,"
  New England Monthly, February 1987

I had already fallen in love with New England. I had made numerous visits there. My own people had come from Vermont and Massachusetts and Connecticut; my boyhood had been full of the stories of the Green Mountain Boys and of the beauties of. . . . Lake Champlain, of maple-sugaring in spring, and the trees hanging full in the autumn with apples and walnuts and chestnuts, of which we in the cold northwest knew nothing.

—RAY STANNARD BAKER,
  American Chronicle, 1945

I'd fight 10,000 devils to save one New Hampshire man!

> —Line by Daniel Webster in *The Devil and Daniel Webster,* 1941 film

As far as I'm concerned, there are exactly two great things about living on the Maine coast in January: 1) empty 2) shrimp.

> —LESLIE LAND,
> *"Everybody Loves Maine Shrimp,"*
> *Yankee* magazine, January 1995

Springfield, Massachusetts, is a place to be from. Talented people ripen in Springfield, then move away to bigger cities to make their fortune.

> —JAMES C. O'CONNELL,
> *Pioneer Valley Reader,* 1995

I think this is the best built and handsomest town I have ever seen. They call New England the land of steady habits, and I can see the evidence about me that it was not named amiss.

> —MARK TWAIN,
> on Hartford, in a letter dated January 25, 1868

There are, generally speaking, five sorts of people found on Cape Cod at one time or another: native residents, natives who are not residents, residents who are not natives, summer residents who are natives, and summer residents who are not natives. A sixth classification . . . is the group known as "guests." Native residents have had company all their lives, as have summer residents who are natives. These hosts are fairly casual about guests, seeing them as a natural and inevitable part of any year—like ticks.

> —MARCIA J. MONBLEAU,
> *The Inevitable Guest: A Survival Guide to Being Company
> and Having Company on Cape Cod*, 2000

[Emily Dickinson] wrote about nature, love, life, death, humanity's relation with God—matters that from time to time occupy the thoughts of all thinking people. But her approach was always that of a New England villager. . . . She wrote that she saw "New Englandly," and she might just as accurately have expressed herself with another coinage, "Amherstly."

—PERRY D. WESTBROOK,
The New England Town in Fact and Fiction, 1989

Once one puts in any amount of time here, one becomes gradually addicted. Eventually, living on the Vineyard becomes a passionate obsession, a religion, a personal identity and a raison d'etre.

—PETER SIMON,
On the Vineyard II, 1990

I know not whether anyone, even in New York, is so hardy as to laugh at Rhode Island, where the spirit of Roger Williams still abides in the very dogs. . . . The small commonwealth, with its stronger and fuller flow of life, is more native, more typical, and therefore richer in real instructions, than the large state can ever be.

—E. A. FREEMAN,
Some Impressions of the United States, 1883

Vern had gone up to the attic to hunt for a fish pole and I trailed along after him. The attic was just like that of any other North Country farmhouse—cobwebby corn, and old clothes; corners piled full of haircloth trunks, boxes, and dead furniture. I saw a home-made cradle, an ancient spinning wheel, a flax-carder, piles of books and magazines and then, suspended from a nail, two pair of river-men's boots. . . . Vern took them in one huge hand and held them almost tenderly. "Those boots, young feller," he said to me, "may be said to mark the passing of an era."

—ROBERT PIKE,
Spiked Boots, 1959

I was watching the ball, of course, so I missed what everyone on television saw—Fisk waving wildly, weaving and writhing and gyrating along the first-base line, as he wished the ball fair, forced it fair, forced it fair with his entire body. . . . I suddenly remembered all my old absent and distant Sox-afflicted friends—in Brookline, Mass., and Brooklin, Maine; in Beverly Farms and Mashpee and Presque Isle and North Conway and Damariscotta; in Pomfret, Connecticut, and Pomfret, Vermont; in Wayland and Providence and Revere and Nashua, and in both the Concords and all five Manchesters; and in Raymond, New Hampshire (where Carlton Fisk lives), and Bellows Falls, Vermont (where Carlton Fisk was born), and I saw all of them dancing and shouting and kissing and leaping about like the fans at Fenway—jumping up and down in their bedrooms and kitchens and living rooms, and in bars and trailers, and even in some boats here and there, I suppose, and on back-country roads (a lone driver getting the news over the radio and blowing his horn over and over, and finally pulling up and getting out and leaping up and down on the cold macadam, yelling into the night), and all of them, for once at least, utterly joyful and believing in that joy—alight with it.

> —ROGER ANGELL,
> *Five Seasons,* 1977

173

Index of Authors Cited

Adams, Henry, 23, 131, 132, 152
Alcott, Louisa May, 38
Aldrich, Thomas Bailey, 140
Allen, Fred, 140
Allen, Henry, 45
Allen, Mel, 119
Ames, Willie, 46
Amory, Cleveland, 139
Angell, Roger, 173

Bachman, Ben, 110
Baker, Ray Stannard, 151, 168
Barrette, Roy, 27
Bates, Katharine Lee, 69
Bearse, Ray, 18
Beecher, Henry Ward, 47, 51, 113, 166
Bell, Michael E., 77
Benchley, Nathaniel, 3
Bernays, Anne, 36
Beston, Henry, 117
Bierce, Ambrose, 44

Blais, Madeline, 52
Blakely, Mary Kay, 92
Bloom, Lary, 93
Boisvert, Donald J., 148
Bossidy, John Collins, 138
Bowles, Ella Shannon, 148, 152, 154, 155
Brann, William Cowper, 132
Brooks, Van Wyck, 12
Brown, Dona, 12
Brown, Richard D., 4
Brunelle, Jim, 56
Bryson, Bill, 100, 101, 102
Burgess, Thornton, 10
Burns, Ken, 164
Burroughs, Franklin, 51

Chandler, Raymond, 132
Chase, Mary Ellen, 113
Chute, Carolyn, 30, 101
Clark, Edie, 36, 81
Clark, Tim, 25

Cleghorn, Sarah N., 160
Cobb, Nathan, 128
Coffin, Robert P. Tristram, 103
Cole, John, 32
Conuel, Thomas, 114
Cooke, Alistair, 52
Coolidge, Calvin, 161, 164
Corbett, Scott, 13
Cowen, Robert C., 30
Cressey, Will M., 18, 35, 58, 79, 85
Crosby, Katharine, 9
Curran, Mary Doyle, 107
Curtis, C. Michael, 63, 67
Curtis, Wayne, 127

Daniels, Jonathon, 60
De Gouy, Louis P., 145, 148
De Voto, Bernard, 6
Delbanco, Andrew, 64
Dietz, Lew, 78
Dodge, Marshall, 75
Dodson, James, 84
Douglass, Fredrick, 59
Drake, Samuel, 123
Dubus, Andre, 127
Durocher, Leo, 60
Dwight, Timothy, 59, 120

Early, Eleanor, 57, 70, 71, 153
Elder, John, 77
Emerson, Ralph Waldo, 92, 110, 133
Erikson, Henry, 44

Farris, Ruth, 43
Finch, Robert, 105
Fitzgerald, F. Scott, 90
Freeman, Castle, Jr., 31, 103, 115
Freeman, E.A., 171
French, Robert Dudley, 114
Frost, Robert, 23, 29, 68, 135, 162

Gardner, John, 70
Garland, Joseph, 106
Garrison, John L., 161
Goodman, Ellen, 89
Gould, John, 27, 79, 84, 151
Grant, Ulysses S., 17
Griffin, Arthur, 38
Gunther, John, 64

Hale, Judson D., Sr., 7, 79, 82, 90, 176
Hall, Donald, 20, 55, 159
Hardwick, Elizabeth, 131

Hart, Jim, 78
Hawthorne, Nathaniel, 68, 100, 102, 111, 121
Hay, John, 99
Heat-Moon, William Least, 5, 55, 104
Hebert, Ernest, 62
Hill, Evan, 45, 70, 76, 90
Hill, Lewis, 57, 63
Hinchman, Walter S., 83
Holmes, Oliver Wendell, 130
Hopper, Edward, 119
Huxtable, Ada Louise, 32

Irving, John, 65, 105, 129

James, Henry, 122, 166
Jones, T. A. D., 95
Junger, Sebastian, 53

Kennedy, John Fitzgerald, 89
Kennedy, Joseph P., 43
Kidder, Tracy, 106
Kingman, Lee, 120
Kipling, Rudyard, 22
Knowles, John, 35, 93, 121
Kramer, Mark, 48, 109

Krutch, Joseph Wood, 39
Kuralt, Charles, 104

Land, Leslie, 169
Langton, Jane, 121
Larcom, Lucy, 49
Leavitt, Robert K., 58
Lewis, Wilmarth S., 91
Lincoln, Joseph C., 145
Lippincott, Bertram, 66
Longfellow, Henry Wadsworth, 139

Mabie, Hamilton Wright, 64
MacLeish, Archibald, 35, 93, 117
Magliozzi, Tom, 94
Mailer, Norman, 21
Malcolm, Andrew H., 47
Mansfield, Howard, 60
Marquand, John P., 68, 128
Marquis, Don, 157
McCord, David, 136
McGrory, Brian, 137
McPhee, John, 33
Melville, Herman, 10
Merrifield, Richard F., 76
Meryman, Richard, 8
Monbleau, Marcia J., 170

Morison, Samuel Eliot, 65
Morrissey, Charles T., 19, 39
Mosher, Howard Frank, 28

Nunan, Bertha, 149
Nutting, Wallace, 9, 37, 108

O'Brien, Tim, 116
O'Connell, James C., 169
Oliver, Mary, 22
Onassis, Jacqueline Kennedy, 94

Parker, Dorothy, 92
Parker, Robert B., 129
Parks, Edwards, 37
Perkins, Maxwell, 11
Perley, Sidney, 34
Perrin, Noel, 62
Peterson, Roger Tory, 123, 162
Pike, Robert, 172
Plath, Sylvia, 22
Pole, Ernest, 26
Priester, John, 135

Reisman, Arnie, 83
Rich, Louise Dickinson, 24
Roberts, Kenneth, 6, 102, 154, 155

Robinson, Edward Arlington, 127
Roth, Philip, 3

Santayana, George, 138
Sarton, May, 164
Sedgwick, John, 51
Shachtman, Tom, 20
Simon, Anne W., 116
Simon, Peter, 171
Skillings, Roger, 101
Slayton, Tom, 7
Smith, Captain John, 107, 167
Smith, Robert, 24
Smith, William Bentinck, 89
Snow, Edward Rowe, 137, 167
Solzhenitsyn, Aleksandr, 165
Stamm, Sara B.B., 150, 152, 153
Stegner, Wallace, 91
Stevens, Henry, 61
Stout, Glenn, 134
Stowe, Harriet Beecher, 5, 48
Styron, William, 165
Sullivan, Jim, 138

Taber, Gladys, 25, 31
Taylor, John I., 136
Thollander, Earl, 46

Thomson, Betty Flanders, 99
Thoreau, Henry David, 112, 118, 136, 159
Thorne, John, 33
Todd, Richard, 168
Tolman, Newton F., 54
Towle, Dorothy S., 148, 149, 152, 154, 155
Tree, Christina, 109, 122
Trillin, Calvin, 150
Twain, Mark, 17, 29, 130, 170

Updike, John, 34, 53, 121, 134, 165

Vivante, Arturo, 26
Vorse, Mary Heaton, 108
Vrettos, Theodore, 107

Ward, Artemus, 82
Washington, George, 60
Webster, Daniel, 90, 160
Wells, H. G., 132
Wells, Julia, 167
Westbrook, Perry D., 49, 171
Wharton, Edith, 4
White, E. B. 19, 50, 80, 141, 163
White, Katharine S., 162
Wideman, John Edgar, 112
Wilder, Thornton, 61, 118
Wilson, Alexander, 67
Wister, Owen, 140
Wyeth, Andrew, 56
Wyss, Bob, 122

Yaro, Robert, 115

p. 170 – 94 – 27 – 28 – 51 – 61 – 29 –
43 – 46 –